WILDLIFE PROJECTS

The Best of **SCROLLSAW**
Woodworking & Crafts Magazine

WILDLIFE PROJECTS

28 Favorite Projects & Patterns

From the editors of
Scroll Saw Woodworking & Crafts

Stalking Leopard Portrait,
page 103

Fox Chapel
PUBLISHING

ISBN 978-1-56523-502-1

Library of Congress Cataloging-in-Publication Data

Wildlife projects / from the editors of Scroll saw woodworking & crafts.

    p. cm. -- (The best of Scroll saw woodworking & crafts magazine)

Includes index.

ISBN 978-1-56523-502-1

1. Fretwork. 2. Jig saws. 3. Woodwork--Patterns. 4. Wildlife art. 5. Wildlife wood-carving. I. Scroll saw woodworking & crafts. II. Title. III. Series.

NK9930.W55 2010

745.51'3--dc22

2010038221

To learn more about the other great books from Fox Chapel Publishing, or to find a retailer near you, call toll-free 800-457-9112 or visit us at *www.FoxChapelPublishing.com*.

Note to Authors: We are always looking for talented authors to write new books in our area of woodworking, design, and related crafts. Please send a brief letter describing your idea to Acquisition Editor, 1970 Broad Street, East Petersburg, PA 17520.

Printed in China
First printing: February 2011

Table of Contents

What You Can Make

Fretwork

Bald Eagle, page 12

Rooster, page 15

Birds, page 20

Boxer, page 34

Horse, page 42

Ocean Scenery, page 56

Fish, page 58

Buffalo, page 72

Bear, page 76

Woodland Shadowbox, page 79

Wolves, page 82

Moose, page 84

Display Shelf, page 88

Grizzly Bear, page 91

Loons, page 94

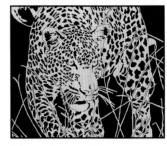
Leopard, page 103

Tiger, page 106

Cheetahs, page 108

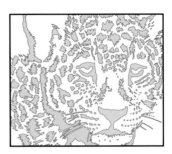
Jaguar, page 110

Intarsia and Segmentation

Rooster, page 15

Blue Jay, page 22

Cat, page 28

Easter Bunny, page 36

Brown Trout, page 46

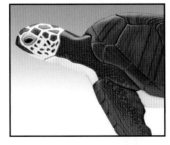
Sea Turtle, page 52

Crab, page 60

Wolf, page 66

Elk, page 68

Lion, page 98

Introduction

Scroll Saw Woodworking & Crafts is proud to present this collection of 28 wildlife projects. This book will enable you to create your own wooden zoo, using your scroll saw to make everything from a sea turtle to an elk to a house cat.

The variety goes beyond kinds of animals, too. Some projects are all about the scroll saw, using only dozens of small cuts on a single piece of wood to form an animal's likeness. Others incorporate different skills, adding multiple woods, sanding, and paint to form multi-dimensional intarsia images.

The categories—Birds, Pets, Water Life, North American Wildlife, and Big Cats—will help you decide which project to tackle first. Most are decorative, designed to be hung on walls, but you will also find a napkin holder, a coat rack, some trivet options, and even one aquatic portrait that can bring new life to an abandoned aquarium.

The more demanding projects include detailed step-by-step instructions, while some of the simpler ones consist only of a pattern and picture of the final project. You will also find tips that will help you improve your skills scattered throughout the book.

Whether you're carving for yourself or as a gift for someone else, we're sure you will enjoy making these wild, wonderful creatures.

Horse, page 42

Birds

From the huge bald eagle to the tiny songbird, birds have always captured the human imagination. We envy their flight, smile at their song, and thrill to the unexpected flash of color they bring the landscape.

The four projects in this section offer a chance to translate that fascination into works of art that make captivating home accents and gifts. Maybe the rooster napkin holder will remind you of all those times you awoke to that early-morning crow, or the blue jay intarsia of the beauties of nature.

Whether you're a seasoned scroller or just starting out, the variety in this set of projects ensures that you will be able to enjoy creating your own fine feathered friend.

Blue Jay Intarsia, page 22

America's Symbol of Freedom

By Leldon Maxcy

Whether you're a beginner or advanced scroller, cutting this eagle project will keep you busy at your saw for some time! You'll get lots of practice making tight turns, which is a great skill to have. Once finished, you will have captured the beauty of this magnificent bird, America's symbol of freedom. This project, cut as a silhouette using oak or a portrait using Baltic birch, should sell well at craft shows.

Step 1: **If you're cutting this as a silhouette and using a hardwood, put 2" packaging tape over the top of the wood.** The tape lubricates the blades and prevents burning. If you're cutting this as a portrait, use ⅛" Baltic birch plywood to stack cut three to six in one cutting session. You can use the packaging tape on the stack too.

Step 2: **Attach the pattern to the wood or to the packaging tape, if you've chosen to apply tape to the wood as described in Step 1.** Use temporary bond spray adhesive. Be sure to spray the back of the paper pattern, NOT the uncovered wood. If you spray the wood, you'll have a hard time removing the pattern.

Step 3: Drill all blade-entry holes with a ¹⁄₁₆" bit. Refer to the pattern and drill in the places marked with X's. Note that all large cuts have at least one drill hole marked. Some of the small interior cuts don't have any drill spots marked. Drill the blade-entry holes in the available space. Keep in mind, too, that you can leave some of these small areas uncut without affecting the overall appearance of the eagle image.

Step 4: Before sawing, sand the back with 180-grit sandpaper to remove any tearout from the drilling. Sanding also evens out the back surface to keep the project level on the saw table.

Step 5: You can leave the corners square or round them as I have in the completed project you see here. If you want to round the corners, do that now, before making any inside cuts. Start cutting out the eagle using the #3 reverse-tooth blade (or blade of choice). As a general rule, cut the smaller inside cuts first so you have more of the workpiece to hold on to as you continue cutting. Periodically sand the back to remove fuzzies to help keep the project level. This might save the fragile pieces from breaking off when you do the final sanding.

Step 6: Remove the pattern. See "What to Do When the Pattern Sticks" if you have difficulty taking it off. After removing the pattern, give the entire piece a good sanding to remove fuzzies and residue left from the spray adhesive. I start with 180-grit sandpaper and finish with 220 grit.

Step 7: Attach the backer. I use a piece of unstained Baltic birch plywood for the backer. Apply and evenly spread the wood glue to the back of the eagle.

Step 8: Apply the finish of your choice. I use four coats of semi-gloss lacquer. If you chose hardwood and you'd like to have a darker finish with more prominent grain, use an oil finish, let it dry one to three days, then apply two or three coats of lacquer. You can frame the one cut as a silhouette, but you would need to cut it the same size of the stack cut ones and use thinner wood.

Photocopy at 110%

Break of Dawn

By Kathy Wise

An ideal partner for your morning coffee, this country rooster is a great way to show off your scrolling skills. The napkin holder is easy to make and can be embellished with fretwork or intarsia. Careful wood selection brings the intarsia version to life, and the project is simple enough to complete in a single day. You can substitute an alternate design to match your décor.

Create matching designs for both sides of the holder by stack cutting. The sections of the intarsia design can be stack cut from ½"-thick wood. The fretwork rooster is stack cut from ¼"-thick stock.

Always keep a master copy of your pattern for later use. Make two copies of the side pattern per napkin holder. For the intarsia overlay, make five copies of the rooster pattern. Cut the pattern pieces apart and

separate them into color groups. You need only one copy of the fretwork rooster. Tape contact paper flat on a board. Spray adhesive on the pattern and position it on the shiny side of the contact paper. Cut the blanks to size according to the materials list.

Make sure all the wood you use is flat. Plane any wood that is not flat, because you must have flat wood to get a tight-fitting intarsia.

TIP SQUARE CUTS

Make sure your blade is square to the saw table by using a square to check a cut piece.

NAPKIN HOLDER: FRETWORK

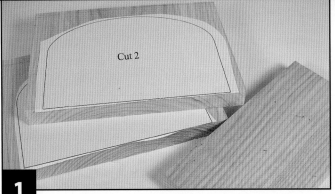

1 **Cut the holder.** Use a #5 skip-tooth blade. Place the bottom of the side patterns on a flat edge to ensure a good joint. Round the edges by sanding them or using your router bit of choice. Do not round the side pieces where they attach to the base. Sand the pieces smooth.

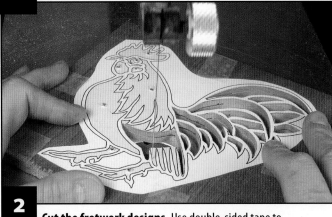

2 **Cut the fretwork designs.** Use double-sided tape to attach two ¼"-thick blanks together. Attach the pattern and drill ⅟₁₆"-diameter blade-entry holes. Sand away any tearout on the bottom. Cut the internal frets first, then cut the perimeter. Separate the stack and sand the wood smooth.

3 **Glue the fretwork to the sides.** Dry fit the rooster to the side piece, and mark the location of the feet with a pencil. Apply dots of clear cyanoacrylate (CA) glue to the back of the roosters and press them in place on the sides. Apply spray varnish to the fretwork, sides, and base.

NAPKIN HOLDER: INTARSIA

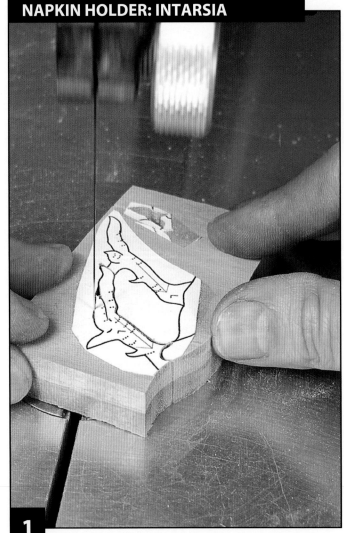

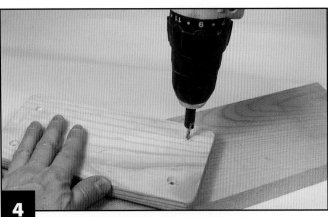

4 **Assemble the holder.** Use a pencil to mark the position of the sides on the base. Drill and countersink four holes in the base. Align the sides and use a nail through the holes to mark the sides. Drill pilot holes on the marks. Apply wood glue to the bottom of the sides and attach them to the base with screws.

1 **Cut the intarsia rooster.** Choose the wood for each section of the rooster. Cut the pieces individually or use double-sided tape to attach two ½"-thick pieces of wood for each section. Stack cutting creates matching overlays for each side. Cut the pieces with a #3 skip-tooth blade. Do not cut the individual feathers yet.

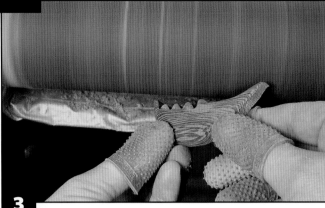

2 **Check the fit of the pieces.** Position the cut pieces on a copy of the pattern. Adjust the fit or recut as necessary. Separate the stacks and use CA glue to attach the two parts of the wing together. Cut apart the individual wing feathers. Reassemble the two roosters.

3 **Sand and shape the pieces.** Use a 2"-diameter pneumatic drum sander and a 220-grit sanding sleeve to shape the larger pieces. Replace the pieces back on the pattern to check the flow and mark the areas to remove. Mark, sand, and replace the pieces as often as necessary.

4 **Add the details.** Use a rotary power carver with a ½"- or ¼"-diameter sanding drum to shape the smaller pieces and add details. Drill a hole for the eye or add a small ebony dowel. Use a carving knife to clean out the cuts on the wings. Add detail to the legs and beak with a wood burner.

5 **Smooth the pieces.** Sand the pieces with a 220-grit or finer sanding mop. This gives the pieces a nice sheen and it removes the scratches from the earlier sanding process. It also produces a smoother surface in preparation for the application of the spray varnish in step 7.

6 **Tack the rooster together.** Use CA glue. Place several dots of glue on one side and spray CA glue accelerator on the side of the adjoining piece. Press them together on a flat surface. Sand the back of the joined pieces to ensure a flat surface. Spray varnish on the sides and tops of the roosters and the base.

7 **Glue the roosters to the sides.** Mark the location of the rooster with a pencil. Apply CA glue to each section of the back of the rooster. Spray accelerator on the side piece. Position the rooster and hold it in place until the glue sets. Apply spray varnish to the side piece. Assemble the napkin holder as in fretwork step 4.

Rooster overlay patterns

Intarsia

Stack cut 2 pieces of ½" wood for each color

Legend

⟵ Grain direction
B........Black or darkest shade
R........Red
M.......Medium rust
L........Light
⌇⌇⌇ Wood burn detail

Wood burn details on feet

Photocopy at 100%

Fretwork

Cut 2

Napkin holder base

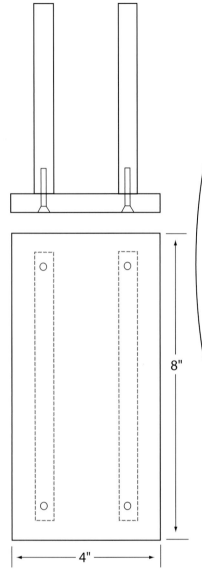

8"

4"

Base assembly

Napkin holder side—cut 2

Birds and Boughs Fretwork

Design by Ellen Brown
Cut by Dale Helgerson

These beautiful songbird scenes are ideal for use as trivets or, grouped, as eye-catching wall displays. Cut them from thin plywood with an acrylic backing for colorful suncatchers.

If you plan to use the projects as trivets, take the finish into consideration. Hot plates will damage most finishes. Aside from two-part varnishes (which can be very difficult to apply), a polyurethane finish is the most heat-resistant. Another option would be to leave the piece unfinished. You can make an unfinished hardwood trivet shine by sanding with progressively finer grits of sandpaper up to 600-grit. Then buff it with 0000 steel wool, or the synthetic alternative.

Photocopy at 100%

Blue Jay Intarsia

By Kathy Wise

Blue jays are one of the most common birds in the United States. Intelligent and adaptable, they take advantage of almost any food source. Blue jays can imitate a variety of sounds—including the scream of a hawk, which is sure to clear the way at the local feeder.

This lively blue jay design is highlighted by the use of blue pine, a piece of yellow pine that was attacked by pinecone beetles, which transmit the blue stain fungus. Blue and gray wood can be difficult to find, so another alternative would be to paint a white wood with a wash of blue acrylic or oil paint. Practice on scrap wood until you are satisfied with the color.

Start by transferring the patterns to the workpiece. Make two copies of the pattern, and always keep a master copy. Cut the pattern pieces, and divide them into groups based on color. Spray adhesive to the back of the pattern pieces, and adhere the pattern to the shiny side of a piece of clear contact paper. Cut each pattern piece from the contact paper. Attach a full-size pattern to contact paper, using the same method. Transfer the full-size pattern to the wood you plan to use as a backing board. The contact paper can be repositioned if needed, and it is easy to remove after cutting.

1 **Choose the wood for each piece.** Stick the pattern pieces onto your stock. Align the grain direction with the arrows. For a good cut and fit, plane any wood that is not flat before you lay out your pattern. Cut large pieces into smaller, manageable pieces.

2 **Cut the pieces.** Make sure your blade is square to the saw table. Carefully cut all of the pieces, using your blade of choice. For the thick pieces, I use a #5 skip-tooth blade. I use a #3 reverse-tooth blade for the cuts between the wings. Leave the feather sections intact for the time being.

3 **Glue the feather sections together.** I use cyanoacrylate (CA) glue. If you need to remove the pattern to check the fit, you can replace it afterwards, or sketch on the individual feathers. Cut out the individual feathers for the wings and tail. Note: on the top wing sections, the white wood is glued only to the gray wood.

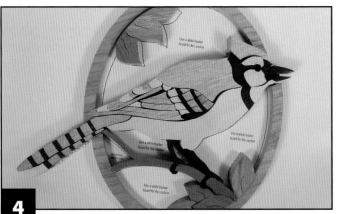

4 **Check the pieces for fit.** Place all of the cut pieces on a pattern adhered to the backing board. Check to see how you like the grain pattern. If you want to make any changes, now is the time to do it. Glue together areas that should be shaped as one piece, such as the head and tail sections. Shim up the breast wing section ¼" before sanding to give the piece more depth.

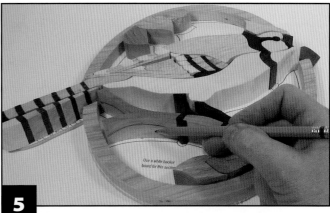

5 **Shape the pieces.** Refer to the shading on the pattern. Pencil in marks as a guide and replace the pieces often to check your progress. Re-mark as needed. I use a pneumatic drum sander and wear rubber fingertips for protection. An air grinder with a ½"-diameter sanding drum works well for the small pieces.

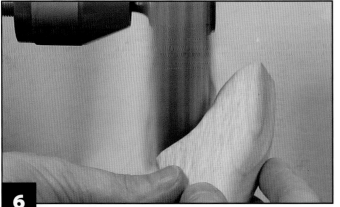

6 **Finish sanding the pieces.** I use a sanding mop. A 120-grit mop rounds the pieces quickly and gets into all of the curves and crevices. Use a light touch with the softer woods. Then switch to a 220-grit mop to put a beautiful sheen on the wood. Dry fit the pieces together and make any adjustments by re-cutting or sanding for a tight fit.

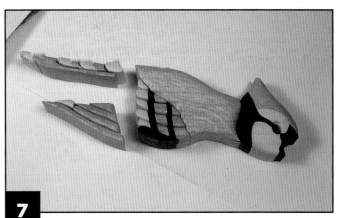

7 **Glue the feathers together.** When you are happy with the fit, glue the feather sections together. For a project with fewer pieces, you can burn the dark stripes onto the feathers with a woodburner. Press the three wing feather sections up against the body, and glue them in place using CA glue. You need a tight fit in these areas.

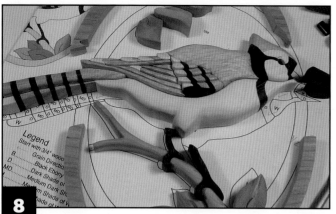

8 **Glue the project together.** I use CA glue and glue accelerator. Position all of the pieces on the full pattern. Glue the bird together first. Then move on to the frame sections, the legs and branches, and the leaves. Apply pressure to make sure you have a flat bottom and a tight fit. Then apply a spray varnish to the entire project. Follow the manufacturer's instructions.

9 **Cut the ¼"-thick backing board.** Place the assembled blue jay on the backer, and trace around the perimeter. Cut along your lines. You can use walnut like in the project, a mirror or colored acrylic, or forego a backing board and leave the piece open for an airy look. If you decide not to use a backing board, be sure to reinforce your glue joints with more CA glue or epoxy. Sand the back before gluing for a tight fit.

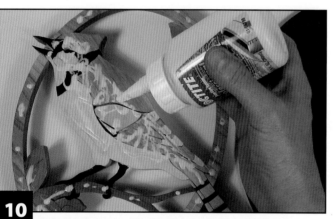

10 **Glue the project to the backing board.** Apply a light but thorough layer of wood glue to the back of the project. I use a few drops of CA glue and accelerator to lock the pieces in place. You could also clamp the pieces together until the glue dries. If any of the wood glue squeezes out, clean it up with a wet cotton swab. Attach a hanger to the back of the piece.

Materials & Tools

Materials:

- ½" x 1" x 1" black ebony or black wood of choice (eye; B)
- 1" x 8" x 5" poplar or white wood of choice (face, body, feathers; W)
- 1" x 5" x 5" walnut, wenge, or dark wood of choice (face, feathers, legs, beak; D)
- 1" x 5" x 5" gray or blue colored wood of choice (may be stained or painted, body, head, feathers; MD)
- ½" x 9" x 13" cherry or medium-colored wood of choice (oval frame; M)
- ¾" x 4" x 4" cherry or medium-colored wood of choice (branch; M)
- 1" x 5" x 5" beech or different medium-colored wood of choice (leaves; M)
- ¼" x 12" x 12" walnut or plywood of choice (backer)
- ¼" x 6" x 6" plywood of choice (shims)

- Clear contact paper
- Spray adhesive
- Wood glue
- Cyanoacrylate (CA) glue and accelerator
- Spray varnish, satin & gloss
- White gel stain
- Hanger of choice
- Wiping rags
- Epoxy

Tools:

- #5 skip-tooth blades or blades of choice
- #3 reverse-tooth blades or blades of choice
- Pneumatic drum sander, air grinder with sanding drum, or sanding tools of choice
- Clamps (optional)

TIP KEEPING WHITE WOOD WHITE

Varnish tends to add a slight yellow tone to white wood. To prevent that, apply one coat of a white gel stain, let it dry a few minutes, and wipe it off with a clean rag. Repeat, then let it thoroughly dry overnight before applying varnish.

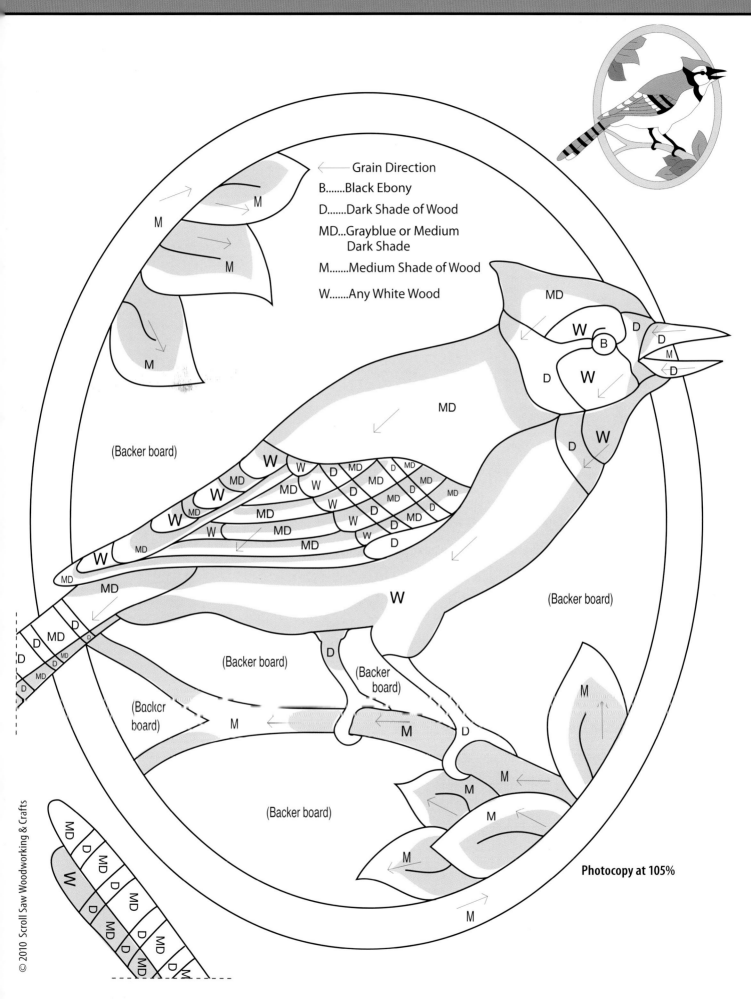

Grain Direction

B.......Black Ebony

D.......Dark Shade of Wood

MD...Grayblue or Medium
       Dark Shade

M.......Medium Shade of Wood

W.......Any White Wood

M

M

M

M

M

(Backer board)

MD

MD

W

W

B

D

D

W

D

W

W

D

W

W

W

MD

MD

MD

D

MD

D

MD

D

MD

D

MD

MD

D

MD

MD

D

MD

D

MD

D

MD

MD

W

W

W

W

D

W

W

D

MD

MD

MD

D

W

MD

MD

MD

MD

D

D

(Backer board)

W

D

MD

D

MD

D

MD

D

D

D

MD

D

MD

(Backer board)

M

(Backer
board)

D

(Backer
board)

M

M

D

M

(Backer board)

M

M

M

M

M

Photocopy at 105%

MD

D

MD

W

MD

D

MD

D

MD

D

MD

D

MD

D

MD

D

W

Pets

Pets are the familiar animals, the ones we love because they have become such a part of our lives. Whether or not you have pets yourself, the four projects in this chapter offer an opportunity to pay artistic tribute to the lives of these four-legged companions.

The furrier animals in this chapter—cat and rabbit—are represented by intarsia. Step-by-step instructions show you how to transform an assortment of woods into finished products so soft, people will want to touch them.

The dog and horse projects take a different tack, using fretwork techniques to produce classic images that, as one designer says, allow viewers' imaginations to fill in the details.

Easter Bunny Intarsia, page 36

Intarsia Cat Portrait

By Janette Square

I was commissioned by a breeder of Ragdoll cats to create a custom portrait of her prized felines. Ragdolls are noted for their "flop in your arms" personality, a gentle and laid-back breed that is both intelligent and good-natured. Ragdolls have gorgeous blue eyes and a beautiful long coat.

This pattern is modified somewhat from the original design to maintain the integrity of the original work.

Use whatever wood you have available. Ragdoll cats come in a wide variety of colors so there is no right or wrong. Wood selection is a personal preference, based on the color and look you want to achieve.

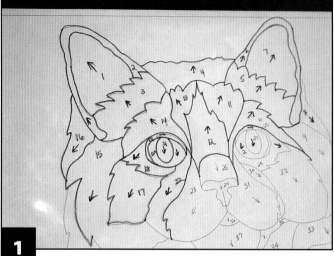

1 **Transfer the pattern onto clear plastic.** The clear pattern enables you to hold it over the wood, slide it around, and select the perfect piece of wood for each section. Mark each corner of the original pattern with an X. Overlay the clear plastic and put an X over the ones you made on the paper pattern; tape the corners down to prevent the plastic from sliding. Trace the pattern and grain direction arrows onto the plastic, using a different color than the paper pattern, so you can see what has already been traced. Number the pieces on both patterns. Choose the wood using the plastic overlay so you can see the grain direction as you select the stock.

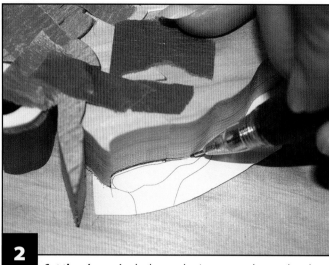

2 **Cut the pieces.** Apply clear packaging tape to the wood, and adhere the paper pattern to the tape with spray adhesive. Cut the piece and sand the bottom to remove any fuzzies. I use the cut and paste method to ensure a tight fit for my pieces. Align the pattern of the next piece you want to cut with the piece you just cut out. Trace the edge of the piece you just cut onto the next pattern piece. Follow this new line when cutting. Work in an outward direction from the bridge of the nose, fitting and taping the pieces together. Cut all of the pieces except for the eyes. Slow down when you have tight curves and let the blade catch up to you as you turn the piece.

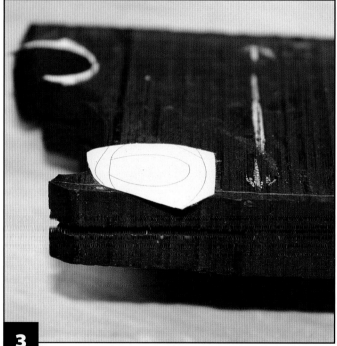

3 **Cut out the pupils.** Once the entire face is cut, cut the eyes. Partially slice a piece of ½"-thick ebony lengthwise. This will give you two identical pupils that are each ¼"-thick. During assembly, attach risers, or shims, to bring the pupils up to the proper height. This saves the amount of ebony you use and ensures that both pupils are the same size. Once the pupils are cut, trace around them onto the pattern for the white part of the eyes. Be sure the pupils are parallel to each other when lining them up to trace. If they are skewed in either direction, the cat may appear cross-eyed. Mark your eyes R and L on the bottom, as it is easy to get them mixed up later on. Check your fit. The eyes are the most important part of the piece.

4 **Add risers to the pupils.** Find a scrap of wood that is the thickness you need, and trace the pupils onto the scrap. Cut inside the line you traced to ensure that the risers do not stick out farther than your piece. Sand off any fuzz; then glue them to the bottom of the ebony. Transfer any numbers or R and L to the bottom of the risers. Wipe off any excess glue, and let them dry for a few minutes.

TIP **AFFORDABLE EXOTIC ACCENT WOODS**

For small pieces of expensive exotic woods, like the ebony I use for the pupil, it really doesn't make sense to buy an entire board. Check your local wood supply store, and see if they have any pen blanks. Often, you can get away with buying a pen blank of exotic wood at a fraction of what a board would cost you. Be sure you know the width of the pieces you need ahead of time, or better yet, take the pattern with you when you go to the store.

5 **Add risers to the rest of the project.** I use ⅛"-thick plywood to raise the nose, the pieces above it, and the round muzzle pieces under the nose. You will eventually be shaping the nose bridge area to taper lower toward the top, so stepping the woods down here will make it a bit easier (the lowest piece being the one at the very top of his head). The front legs should be about ⅛" higher than the back.

TIP **BLUE PINE**

When working with this beautiful wood, it is important to check for tiny bug holes in the wood. Be sure to check both sides. It's a good idea to stick a small nail or tool into the hole to see how deep and what direction it goes. Keep this in mind when placing your pattern to avoid surprises when you begin shaping.

Shaping

Before you start shaping, keep this in mind: cat's noses stick out farther than their foreheads (unless they're Persian), but if you look at them in profile, their eyes are recessed a bit back from the forehead. Their cheekbones are usually quite pronounced. It is difficult to give this illusion when shaping a cat face head-on. I suggest you look at some pictures or your own cat, if you have one.

6 **Shape the face.** The areas around the nose and eyes are the trickiest parts to shape. I go back to this area several times as I shape the adjoining pieces. The white blaze above the nose and the gray piece above it should be rough-shaped together; you can also add the top piece as well. Tape them together, and use a scrap piece of ¼"-thick plywood, or whatever you have on hand, to keep the pieces even on the bottom.

7 **Rough shape the pieces.** I use a 180-grit sanding sleeve on a flexible-drum sander attached to a drill press. Work your way around the face, paying particular attention to the area around the eyes and nose. After shaping one piece, draw a line onto the side of the adjacent piece to indicate your stopping point. This will ensure that each piece aligns with the next. When shaping the nose, angle the bottom of the piece so it is lower than the top. Again, leave the nose slightly higher than the next piece, and adjust it later while doing your hand work.

8 **Shape the ears.** The inside pieces should be slightly concave and lower than the adjoining head pieces. I use a spindle sander. Move the piece back and forth, making a scoop wider at the base and narrower at the top. Don't round over the edges of these pieces. The ears should be symmetrical. For the outer portion of the ear, sand close to the line you drew from the adjoining earpiece, but not all the way to it. Round over the outside ear pieces where they don't meet other pieces. The ears should be slightly higher than the face. Hand sand the inside portion of the outer ear pieces to round them over and line up with the inner pieces.

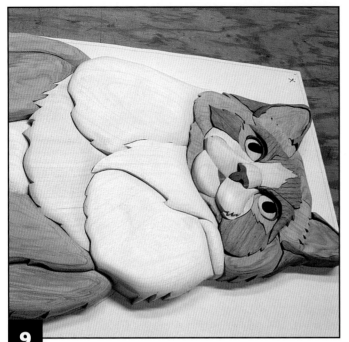

9 **Shape the rest of the cat.** Sand the pupil and the white areas together, going in a soft back and forth motion with the grain to give them a slightly rounded appearance. After this, lightly sand just the white area to remove the black dust. Do not rough sand the small dark brown pieces above the eyes. Shape these sections by hand in step 10. Move on to the chest area. Each piece should be lower at the top and flare at the bottom. This is done to show the fluffiness of the cat. Make the top of the chest pieces lower than the face pieces, gently curving them. Round over the edges where no pieces adjoin on either side. Draw lines where other pieces meet up to avoid rounding over where you shouldn't. Taper the top of the left chest piece where it comes up to meet the face to give the appearance of it disappearing behind the cat's head. The lower piece between the front legs represents the cat's tummy, which should be thinner than the front legs and chest. The feet should appear slightly higher than the legs and rounded. Feather the tail in the same manner as the chest to give it a fluffy look.

TIP **THE "V" FACTOR**

Don't be intimidated by all of the pointy cuts—fondly referred to as "V's". I find that the biggest culprit for "less than tight fits" when doing long-haired animals is that the V cuts aren't quite deep enough to accommodate the matching point. If you find this, an extra nip with the blade, making the V slightly deeper, helps. You can tell which V you need to deepen by holding the two adjoining pieces together. You can also shorten the point of the opposite piece just a hair. This will usually make a huge difference in the fit.

10 **Sand the pieces with a 220-grit sanding sleeve.** Sand with the grain to remove any scratches. Add more curves to some of your edges, but watch the adjoining pieces. Then hand sand each piece to ease the sharp edges. I use an old sanding sponge with a piece of 220-grit sandpaper. Fold the two together like a piece of bread. Remove any sharp edges, fine tune where pieces meet, and soften the overall look of the piece. For tight areas that the sponge won't fit, wrap the sandpaper around your finger or some other small tool.

11 **Paint the eyes.** Mix acrylic paint or watercolors with water, and test the color on some scrap wood of the same variety used for the eyes. A ragdoll cat's eyes vary in shade, but are always blue. Let the paint soak in for a minute or so to see what they will look like. I recommend applying two coats. Experiment with different shades until you find one you are happy with. Be sure to mix enough paint to cover both eyes at the same time, so their color is uniform. Allow the eyes to dry before gluing.

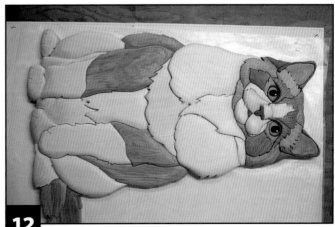

12 **Glue up the project.** Re-assemble your project on a copy of the pattern covered with wax paper. Use a wooden skewer to apply glue to the sides of the pieces. Begin by gluing the pieces that interlock tightly (such as the ears) and work your way down the project. Carefully lift individual pieces out, glue the sides of adjoining pieces, and slide the pieces back in. Use a sharp toothpick to apply a small dot of antique white acrylic paint to each eye for the highlight. Allow it to dry for several hours.

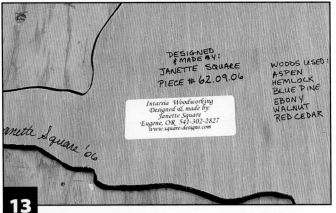

13 **Prepare the backing board.** I use ⅛"-thick lauan door skin. Trace your glued project onto the "bad" side of the board, using a pencil. Using a #2 or #3 blade, cut about ⅛" inside the perimeter of the lines. Ignore the Vs and small indents, and keep softer curves if possible. Sand both sides and the edge of the backing board with a 220-grit sanding sleeve on a flexible-drum sander. Bevel the edges back to soften them. Hand sand all of the edges and bevel any areas where the sander didn't reach. Use a wide black permanent marker to draw around the edges. This helps the backer to disappear when mounted on the wall. List all of the woods used, assign a piece number, and sign your name on the backing board.

14 **Apply the clear satin gel varnish.** Clear the dust on the piece. Apply the gel with a 1" foam brush. Start with the edges all the way around, then move on to the surface. Apply it liberally for the first coat, so it can soak into the wood. Ensure that all of the nooks and crannies are covered. If any areas begin to dry before you finish, simply go back over them with your brush. Once the entire piece is coated, wipe off the excess. Hold the piece up to the light at an angle, looking at it from all directions to see if there are any missed spots. Allow your project to dry overnight. Repeat the process for the second coat. I use an air compressor to blow out the gel from the cracks and crevices. A pointed tool cushioned by paper towels is also handy.

15 **Attach the backer.** Dry fit the backer in place to ensure a good fit. Make any adjustments necessary. Use a glue brush to apply a thin layer of wood glue to the front of the backer. Lay your project face down on a soft surface. Old clothes or clean rags work well. Lay the backer onto the piece, wiggling it around slightly to ensure good glue contact. Check for overhang and adjust as necessary. Place several clamps around the piece. I use clean, old socks to protect the piece from the clamps. Continue working your way around several times, adding clamps, until there are no gaps between the piece and the backer. Wipe away any glue squeeze-out. Allow the project to dry. Attach a hanger to the back to complete the project.

Materials & Tools

Materials:
- Woods used: Aspen (white parts of cat), Blue pine (gray areas around face and tail), Hemlock (outer areas of face and tan parts), Walnut (dark areas around eyes), Ebony (pupils), Tennessee red cedar (nose and mouth). I used Pink Ivory on the custom piece.
- ⅛" lauan door skin or Baltic birch plywood for backing board
- Clear packaging tape
- Fine point permanent marker
- Sharp pencil
- Blue painter's tape
- Carbon or tracing paper (to trace patterns onto wood) or temporary-bond spray adhesive and several copies of the pattern
- Clear plastic cellophane or heavyweight clear plastic
- 180- & 220-grit sanding sleeves
- Sandpaper, 220-grit
- Yellow wood glue with skewers to apply
- Wax paper

- Watercolor or acrylic paints to color eyes blue
- Antique or off-white acrylic paint for the highlight in the eyes
- Clear satin gel varnish
- Wide tip black permanent marker to draw around finished edge of backer

Tools:
- #7 and #2 or #3 reverse-tooth premium blades
- Drill press with flexible-drum sander
- Oscillating spindle sander
- Old sanding sponge to act as sanding block
- Paintbrush
- Foam brushes
- Miscellaneous small, dental tools or wood skewer (to remove varnish from cracks)
- Air compressor (to remove varnish and sawdust from cracks, optional)

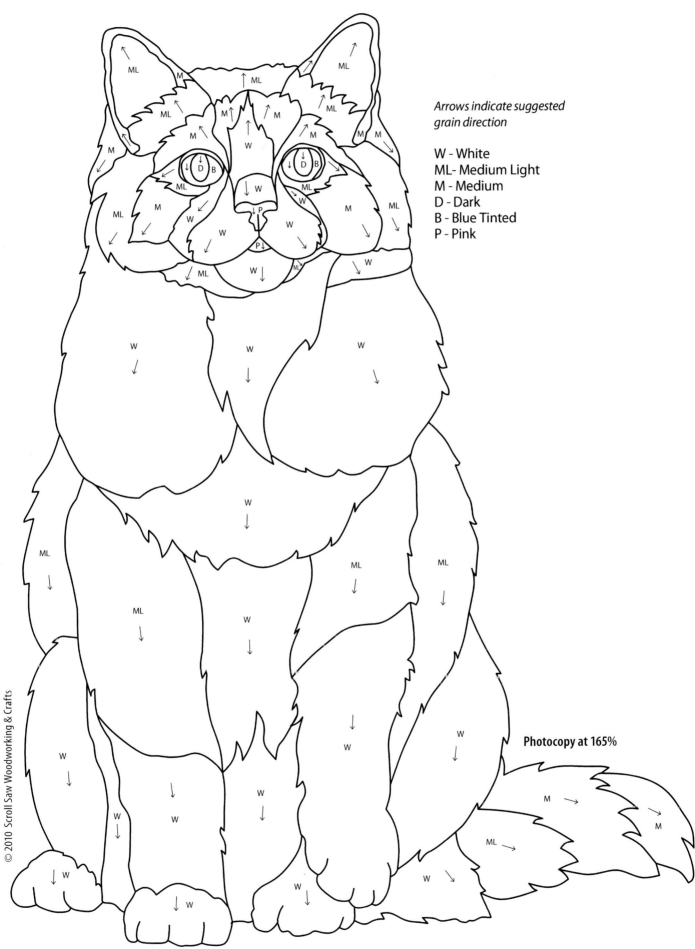

Arrows indicate suggested grain direction

W - White
ML- Medium Light
M - Medium
D - Dark
B - Blue Tinted
P - Pink

Photocopy at 165%

© 2010 Scroll Saw Woodworking & Crafts

Man's Best Friend

By Harry Savage

People like dogs, so I've designed this eye-catching portrait of a boxer that has sold well at shows. I needed to use only a #⅖ reverse-tooth blade to create this canine.

Step 1: **Glue and center the pattern on plywood using temporary bond spray adhesive.**

Step 2: **Using a #60 bit, drill the blade-entry holes into waste areas, which are dark on the pattern.**

Step 3: **Before sawing, sand the back with 180-grit sandpaper to remove any tearout from the drilling.** Sanding also evens out the back surface to keep the project level on the saw table.

Step 4: **Using a #⅖ reverse-tooth blade, cut out the black areas starting in the center for easier handling of the piece.** Once the cutting is complete, remove the dust with an air blower or a tack rag to be sure all the dust is removed.

Step 5: **Spray the piece with a clear coat finish spray.** Allow sufficient time for the spray to dry.

Step 6: **Use tacky glue to adhere the black felt to the back of the cutout pattern.**

Step 7: **Attach a sawtooth hanger to the middle top back of the frame.**

Step 8: **Insert the portrait into an 11" x 14" frame.**

Materials & Tools

Materials:
- ⅛" x 14" x 11" Baltic birch plywood
- Sandpaper, 180 and 220 grits
- 11" x 14" wood frame
- 1 piece, 8" x 10" black felt material for the background
- Temporary bond spray adhesive
- Clear coat finish spray
- Tack rag

Tools:
- #2/0 reverse-tooth blade
- Drill with #60 bit
- Tacky glue

Photocopy at 100%

Easter Bunny Intarsia

By Kathy Wise

This versatile design can be made a number of different ways. First choose whether your bunny will be a solid color or have spots. Then decide if you will display the bunny on its own, add the simple base, or include the Easter egg design.

The project is actually very easy to cut and assemble. In fact, the solid color bunny has only 23 pieces. Try experimenting with different woods or stains to create your very own design.

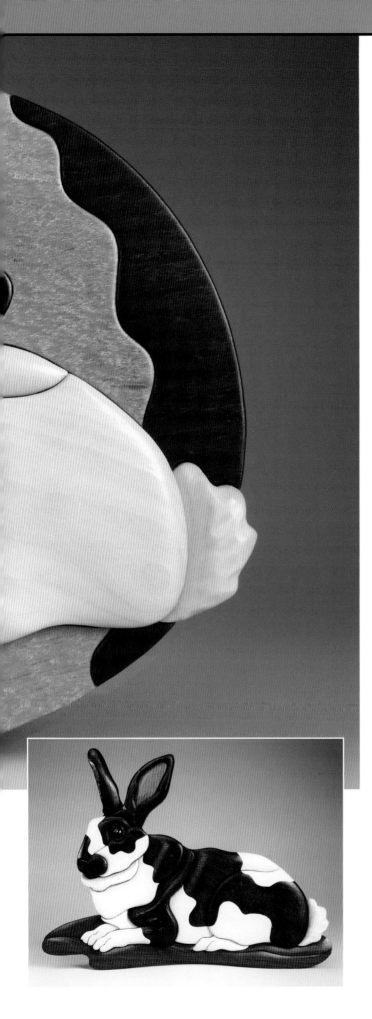

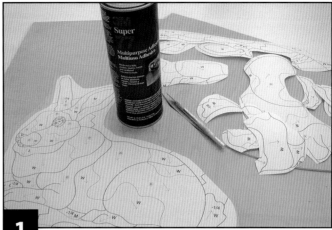

1 **Prepare your pattern.** Make eight copies of the pattern. Always keep a master copy. Cut out and group the pattern pieces together by color. Apply spray adhesive to the back of your pattern pieces, and stick them to the shiny side of the clear contact paper. The contact paper sticks well to the wood and is easy to remove.

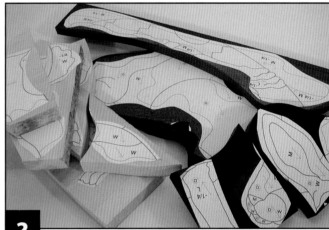

2 **Attach the pattern pieces to the wood.** Cut out each pattern piece. Use a full-size pattern as a layout board and later to cut out your backing board. Peel and stick the pattern pieces onto your selected pieces of wood. Be sure to line up the grain direction.

3 **Cut out all the pieces.** It is important to start with flat wood for a good cut and fit. Plane any wood that is not flat before you begin. Make sure your blade is square to the saw table by using a square to check a cut piece. Use a #5 reverse-tooth blade, or your blade of choice.

4 **Check the pieces for fit.** Place all of the cut pieces on a pattern taped to a work board, and check them for fit. Also check to see how you like the grain pattern and the colors of the wood you have picked. Make any adjustments needed. If you want to make any color or grain direction changes, this is the time!

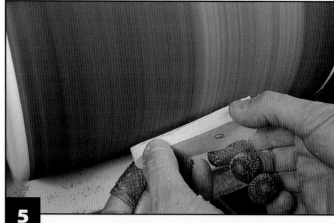

5 **Shape and sand the pieces.** Start with the shaded areas on the patterns and mark any additional areas you want to taper or sand down. Use a pencil. Replace the pieces often to check how much wood you are removing, and remark as needed. I use a pneumatic drum sander and wear rubber finger tips to protect my fingers.

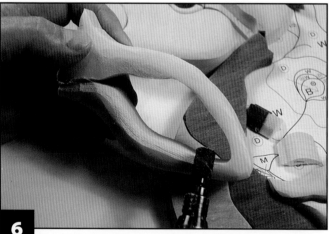

6 **Round the edges.** I use a ¼"-diameter sanding drum in an air grinder to round the inside edges of the ear, which I couldn't reach with the drum sander. Use a hobby knife or your tool of choice to clean out the cuts and add depth to the lines near the ear and between the toes.

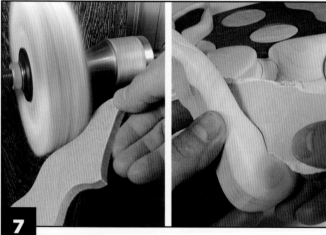

7 **Finish sanding each piece.** I use a sanding mop. It works quickly and gets into all of the curves and crevices. It also puts a nice sheen on the wood. Use a small piece of fine sandpaper to sand between the toes, around the ears, and any other areas that need individual attention.

Making the eyes look alive

I use black ebony for the eyes in my project. The black wood makes the animals seem alive. I put a gloss finish on the eyes and apply a satin finish on the rest of the animal. The gloss reflects the light and makes the eyes look real. I also put a white highlight in each eye. Drill a hole, insert a white wood dowel, and glue it in place with instant glue. When you sand it down, it will look like the reflecting light is hitting the glossy eye. Black ebony is a very hard wood; if you don't want to use it, or can't get it, you can get the same results by staining, painting, using a back permanent marker, ebonizing, or burning the wood. I use thinner pieces of black ebony, which are easier to cut and less expensive to buy. Glue the ebony to a shim with wood glue.

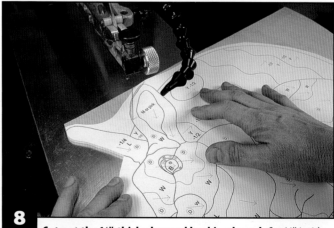

8 **Cut out the ¼"-thick plywood backing board.** Cut ¼" inside the outside perimeter lines of a full-size pattern. Mark the glue side with a marker. Stain the edges of the board dark. Sand the glue side, and remove any stain that may have gotten on the face of the board.

9 Apply the finish. To keep the white rabbit from turning yellow, rub a coat of white gel stain on just the white wood and let it dry overnight. Using a soft clean rag, apply a clear gel varnish to the top and side edges of all the pieces. Let it dry for a few minutes, and wipe it off with a clean rag. Let it dry according to the manufacturer's instructions, and apply a second coat, using the same techniques. Allow the pieces to dry overnight. A clear spray varnish works as well.

10 Assemble the sections. Tack sections together so it is easier to glue them onto the backing board. Place the section on a pattern to make sure they fit tightly together when gluing the pieces together. Sometimes I will glue sections together with instant glue. If you want more flexibility in fitting the pieces when gluing, use 100% silicone glue. Let the silicone dry overnight before gluing. If you have any problems or gaps, simply pull apart the sections, and space them out to hide the open areas.

11 Glue the pieces to the backing board. Don't apply the glue too thickly, or it will come up between the pieces and be impossible to clean up. I use sandbags to weight down the pieces, but it is also possible to clamp the pieces to the backing board.

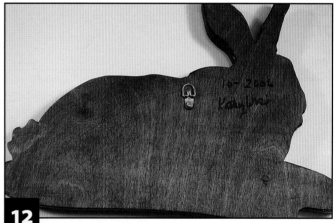

12 Complete the project. Let the glue dry overnight. Trim away any backing board that shows. Then retouch the trimmed areas with stain. Attach the hanger to the back to complete the project. Always remember to sign and date your work.

Materials & Tools

Materials:
- ¾" x 8" x 12" wenge or dark wood of choice (B&W only)
- ¾" x 8" x 24" poplar or white wood of choice (less for B&W)
- ¾" x 3" x 3" pink ebony or pink wood of choice
- ¾" x 3" x 3" ebony or dark walnut (eye)
- ¼"-½" x 8" x 12" yellowheart (egg) (solid only)
- ¼"-½" x 8" x 12" purpleheart (egg) (solid only)
- ¼" -½" x 4" x 18" bloodwood or red wood of choice (base) (B&W only)
- White wood dowel (highlight in eye)
- Roll of clear shelf contact paper
- Spray adhesive
- Wood glue or glue of choice
- 100% silicone glue

- Gel natural varnish or spray varnish
- White-base gel varnish
- Wiping rags
- Hanger

Tools:
- #5 reverse-tooth blades or blades of choice
- Drill with ³⁄₁₆"-diameter bit (for eye, see sidebar)
- Pneumatic drum sander or sander of choice
- Rotary power carver or air grinder with ¼"-diameter sanding drum
- Hobby knife or carving tools of choice

Legend

Start with ¾" wood

← Grain direction

B.............Black ebony /darkest shade

M............Medium shade of wood

L.............Light or white wood

W............Any white wood

P.............Purpleheart or stain

Y.............Yellowheart or stain

-¼.........Sand or plane down ¼"

+¼.........Use ¼" thicker wood

-½.........Plane down ½" or use ¼" wood

Ⓓ ....Dark spots for black & white rabbit

⋯ ....Use for base and black spots only

M or pink

Photocopy at 125%

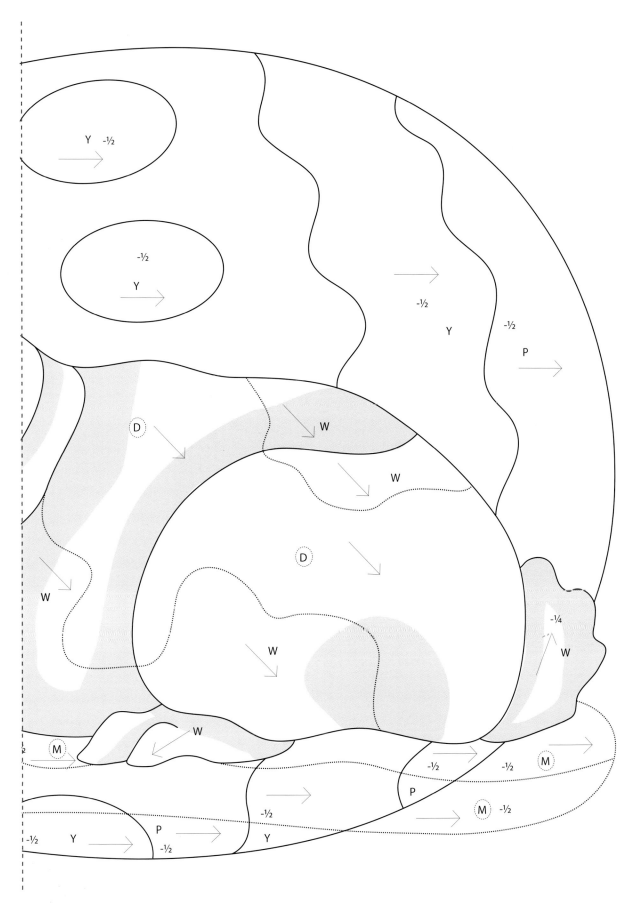

Horse

By Gary Browning

Some things left at their most basic, like the horse pattern, hold a beauty all their own. Everyone sees things differently. Leaving out a few details can add more interest to the portrait. Viewers can fill in those areas with their own idea of how something looks or how a shape represents an object. Your mind automatically fills those areas in because you have seen them over and over. More attention to detail is needed if the subject is not a common scene, object, or person. I like to make patterns of animals and I had a ball doing the horse!

Photocopy at 100%

Water Life

Fun, colorful, mysterious—water and its creatures are all this and more. Maybe that's why these animals so often star in tales of sport and adventure.

These five projects will allow you to capture the spirit of the water and its inhabitants much closer to home—in your workshop.

If you like intarsia, the sea turtle and crab may catch your fancy. For a simple project that will add spice to your aquarium, take a look at On The Ocean Floor. And if what you really want is a fish to hang on your wall, we have two: a traditional scroll saw portrait, and a "scrollsaic" pattern that will give you a chance to use some paintbrushes too.

Build a Realistic Crab, page 60

Brown Trout

By Neal Moore

Trout anglers are gearing up for opening day, but not everyone catches a "wall hanger"—so I decided to work up a fish project you can keep for yourself or give to a fishing buddy. Much like the "one that got away" story, you can make this one as big as you want!

You can cut it any size you desire. It may be necessary to edge glue two or more boards together to get the stock dimensions you need if you go over 12" wide. Be sure to read through the directions before actually starting the project to get a feel for how you will proceed. It's not a difficult project, but planning the cuts in advance can eliminate a lot of frustration.

> **TIP**   **EASY CLEANUP**
>
> *Tape down butcher's paper (waxed side down) and a couple of layers of paper towels to provide an absorbent work surface and a place to dry stained segments. When finished, just discard the entire mess.*

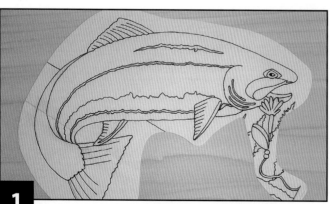

1   **Prepare the pattern and blank.** Trim around the pattern leaving about a ¾"-margin outside the lines. Spray a light coat of temporary-bond adhesive on the back of the pattern, and press it onto the wood. Smooth out any air bubbles so the pattern doesn't lift while you're cutting. Don't spray adhesive directly onto the wood—that keeps the wood from staining evenly and makes it harder to remove the pattern.

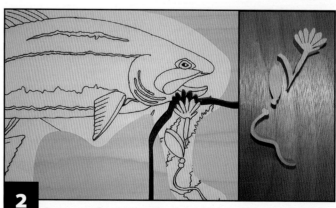

2   **Start your first cut on the right side of the board.** Continue the cut under the trout's lower jaw, and follow the pattern lines along the top of the lure. Exit the cut as shown above. Then cut the lure. Separate the lure into sections as shown above.

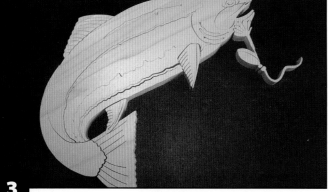

3 **Cut out the remaining segments.** Start by cutting around the margin outside the pattern lines to eliminate the outside waste wood and make the project easier to manipulate on the saw table. Drill blade-entry holes for the inside cuts in the eye, gills, and white highlight on the upper body. Cut out all the inside cuts. Follow the pattern lines, and cut out the remaining segments. Cut the fins and tail first. When all segments are cut, assemble the project for staining.

4 **Stain the fins.** First, assemble the materials you will need for staining. Remove all the project segments that are to remain unstained and place them aside. Refer to the color reference photo often to see how the shading of individual segments should look in the completed project. Dip the top fin in golden oak.

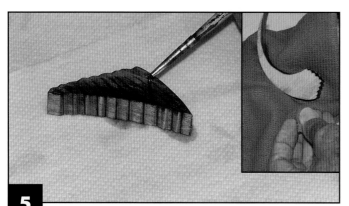

5 **Detail the fin.** While the golden oak stain is still wet, spread dark walnut along the bottom edge, and pull it toward the top edge with a small brush to create a dark to light transition. Checking the reference photo, stain the remaining fins and the tail in the same manner. Place these pieces aside to dry. Stain the curved base of the tail. Apply the golden oak stain, and wipe most of it off. Place this aside to dry.

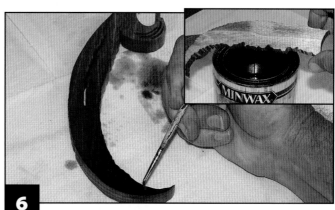

6 **Stain the head and back segment heavily with golden oak.** Use the same technique explained in Step 5 to create a dark to light transition from the tail toward the head using dark walnut. Place this aside to dry. Then stain the next large segment in the fish's body heavily with golden oak. Place it aside to dry.

7 **Stain the next segment of the body with golden oak, and wipe most of it off.** Do the same with the fish belly segment. Place these aside to dry. The two long thin segments that separate the larger body segments are stained dark walnut and placed aside to dry. Stain the eyeball very dark walnut (black). Add a drop of white acrylic when dry. Stain the inner eye ring golden oak and the outer ring dark walnut. Use the acrylic colors recommended or colors of your choice to paint the fishing lure and line. The line can be left natural wood or painted white.

8 **Add the details to the fish's back.** Start by assembling the segments. Use colonial maple stain and a small brush. Highlight the fins, tail, belly, and middle of the fish's body. Dry brush the colonial maple on by dipping the brush in the stain and then wiping most of it off on a paper towel. Keep dry brushing until you achieve the effect you like. Using a small brush and dark walnut, add the dark spots. Use the reference photo as a guide. Follow the color layering techniques explained in the sidebar.

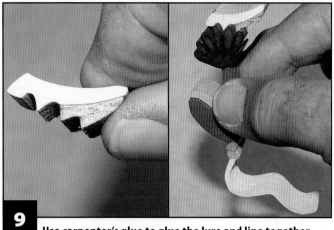

9 **Use carpenter's glue to glue the lure and line together.** Then glue the lower lip and lower jaw together, as shown, using the same techniques. Finally, glue the lip to the lure using carpenter's glue. Place this assembly aside, because it is very fragile and will be the last step in final assembly.

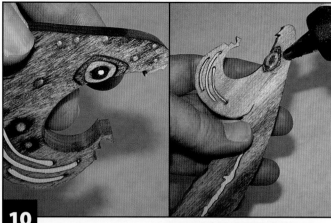

10 **Assemble the three eye segments and fit them into place as shown.** The whole three-piece assembly should be elevated slightly so it resembles the contours of a real fish's eye. While holding the eye in position, turn the piece over and hot glue it in place. Insert the three gill segments and the natural wood-colored highlight segment, and glue them in at this time also. I elevated these pieces about 1/16" for visual interest.

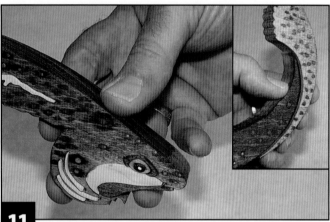

11 **Position the cheek and mouth segments at the same elevation as the eye.** Then hot glue the segments in place. Elevate the curved base of the tail about 1/8" above the main part of the body. Run a bead of hot glue down the center of the back of the joint. The glue will grab both sides of the joint, similar to the "filet weld" metalworkers use to join two pieces of metal.

12 **Position the long, thin strip and the next segment down.** The large segment should be positioned about 3/32" lower than the head and gill as shown in the photo. The thin strip should be elevated about 1/16". Hot glue these to the main body while holding them in position.

13 **Position the next lower body segment about 1/8" lower than the last.** Turn it all over and hot glue it in place. Place the last thin strip and belly segment in position. Hold the belly about 3/32" lower than the last segment, and hot glue it.

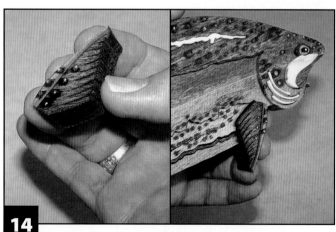

14 **Glue the two pieces of the front fin together with carpenter's glue.** Position the fin so it is elevated about 1/8" above the surface of the body, and hot glue it in.

15 **Position the tail segment about ⅛" higher than the base of the tail.** Glue it in place with carpenter's glue. At this point, the tail should actually be curling out away from the body.

16 **Hot glue the small insert segment in the lower fin.** Now position the fin in place between the body and the tail, as shown, and hot glue it in. Then glue the top fin in place using carpenter's glue.

17 **Place the lower jaw and lure in position.** Glue them in using carpenter's glue. I put the trout on a ¼" lauan backer that I painted light blue and framed it in a poplar frame stained golden oak. The inside dimensions of the frame are about 8½" x 12½". This would also look good displayed on an oval basswood slab or a nice piece of driftwood.

Materials & Tools

Materials:
- ½" x 12" x 14" soft, light wood of choice
- Golden oak, colonial maple, and dark walnut wood stain
- Acrylic art paint in yellow, red, green, white, and gold
- Materials of choice for mounting and displaying the finished project
- Carpenter's glue
- Glue sticks

Tools:
- #3 reverse-tooth blades or blades of choice
- Hot glue gun
- Small art brushes and disposable brushes for painting and staining

Layering colors for the spots

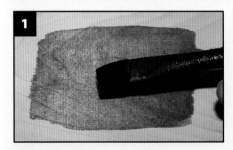

1 **Start by staining the area golden oak.** Allow this to dry.

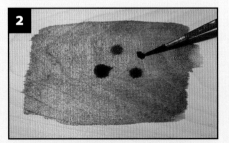

2 **Add a few small spots of dark walnut.** Use a small art brush. Add more stain as needed to make the spots larger or darker. Use care because the stain tends to spread rapidly. Let the spots dry for an hour.

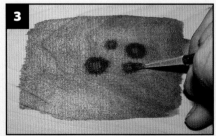

3 **Add the spot of orange.** Make a fairly thin wash of acrylic paint and water. Place a small spot of orange color inside the dark spots. It may be necessary to go back over the orange spots to build the intensity of color. Don't put the orange spots exactly in the center of the dark spots. When the orange acrylic has dried, randomly place small yellow spots over some of the orange as shown in the reference photo.

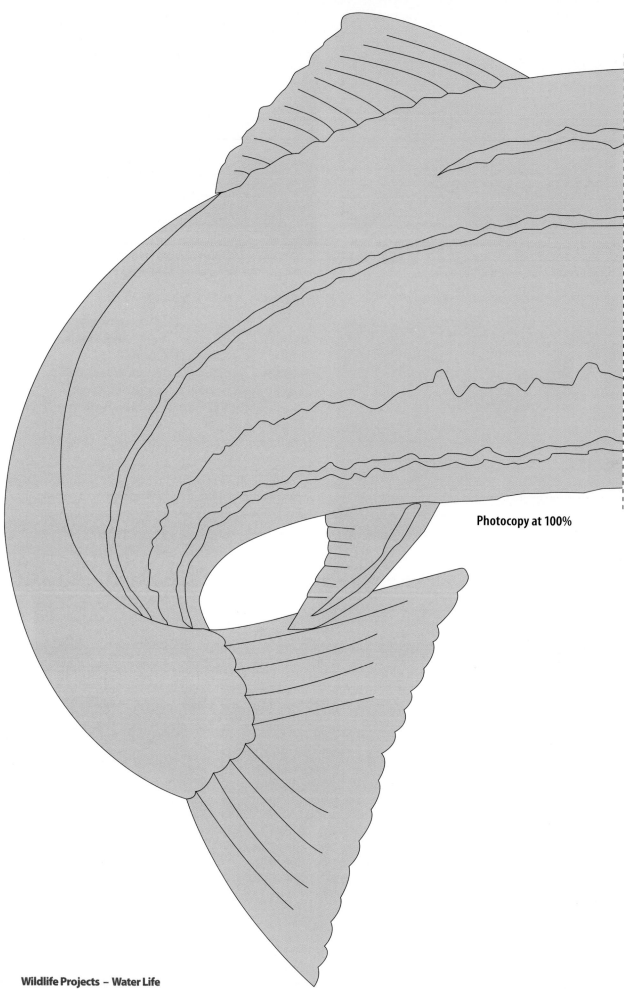

Photocopy at 100%

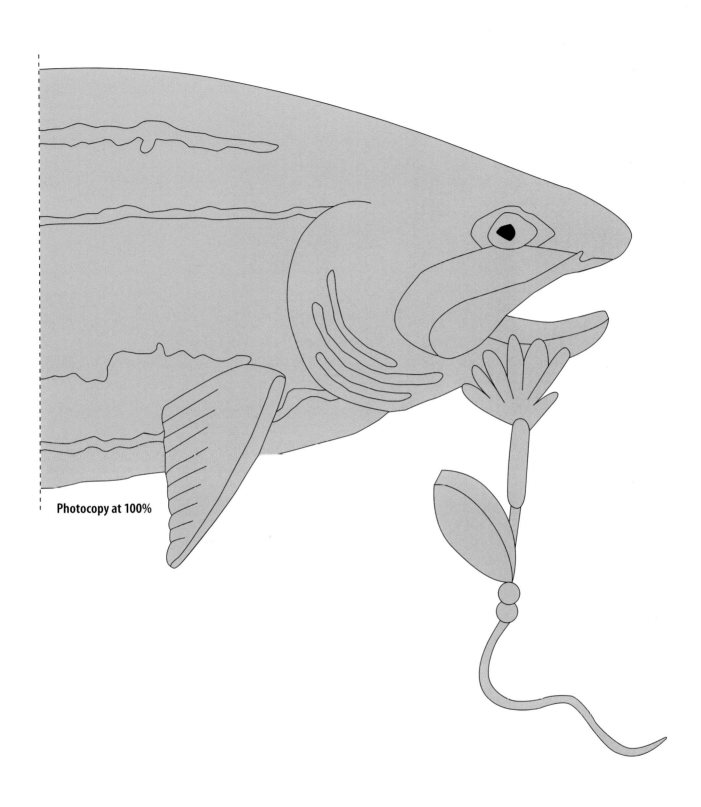

Photocopy at 100%

Sea Turtle Intarsia

By Tim Rogers

The idea of designing a sea turtle intarsia pattern rolled around in my head until I found some lacewood at a wood store. The lacewood reminded me of the pattern on the sea turtle's skin and inspired me to design a pattern.

I first thought about creating a sea turtle in intarsia after my wife and I visited the recently opened Georgia Sea Turtle Center. The center provides state-of-the-art emergency care to sick and injured sea turtles. Although loggerhead turtles are more common to the coast of Georgia, I created a pattern for a green sea turtle.

To get started, transfer the pieces of the pattern to your selected woods. The figure of the wood plays an important part in this design, so choose your wood carefully. After cutting the pieces, divide the turtle into four sections for sanding purposes: the head and neck, shell, front fin, and back fin.

Position the pieces of each section on a scrap of plywood and trace around the perimeter with a pencil. Cut just inside the line and attach the pieces to the sanding shim with light-traffic double-sided carpet tape. Cut a sanding shim for each section so you can contour the entire section as one unit.

After shaping, pry the pieces off the sanding shims with a thin metal putty knife. Hand sand each piece using 220-grit 3X sandpaper. Sand with the grain of the wood. Draw in the areas to be woodburned on the head with a pencil and follow along the pencil lines with a woodburner. Sand the pencil marks off when you have finished burning the designs.

To create a backing board, assemble the turtle on a piece of ¼"-thick plywood and trace around the perimeter with a pencil. Cut just inside the traced line. Sand and paint the edges with black acrylic paint and a 1"-wide sponge brush.

Once the paint dries, sand any excess paint from the back side of the backer board. Do not sand the side you will be gluing to the project. Glue the pieces to the backing board using tacky glue.

Blow the dust off the project with an air compressor. Wipe down the project with a tack-free paper towel and blow it off again. Spray the entire project with clear semi-gloss lacquer and let it dry overnight. Sand the lacquer, going with the grain, using a 320-grit foam sanding pad. Use the air compressor to blow the dust away, wipe it with a paper towel, and

blow the dust away again. Shake the polycrylic can for three to five minutes. It needs to be well mixed or it tends to glob as it sprays out of the can. Spray a light coat of polycrylic on the entire project. The polycrylic has a white sheen when first applied, but will dry clear. Apply a second coat of polycrylic after waiting the recommended time between coats. Apply a third coat if desired. Polycrylic is self-leveling, so do not sand between coats.

Materials & Tools

Materials:
- ¾" x 6" x 48" medium brownish-red wood such as Western red cedar (shell, fin edges, and spots on head)
- ¾" x 3" x 3" light brownish-red wood such as Western red cedar (eye area)
- ¾" x 6" x 12" white wood such as aspen (belly, neck, and head)
- ¾" x 2" x 2" dark wood such as ebony (eye)
- ¾" x 6" x 24" medium-light figured wood such as lacewood (neck, fins, and nose)
- ⅛"-thick scrap plywood (riser for eye area)
- ¼" x 36" x 48" lauan or Baltic birch plywood (backer board and sanding shims)
- Repositionable glue stick
- Clear packing tape
- 2" light-traffic double-sided carpet tape (secure pieces to sanding shims)
- Tacky glue
- Black acrylic paint (backer board edges)
- 100- and 220-grit sanding sleeves with pad (if using flexible-drum sander)
- 220-grit 3X sandpaper
- 320-grit sanding sponge (sand lacquer finish)
- Spray lacquer & polycrylic or finish of choice
- Hanger
- Tack-free paper towels

Tools:
- #1 and #5 reverse-skip tooth blades or blade of choice
- Variable or low-speed bench grinder with flexible-drum sander or sander of choice
- Woodburner (optional)
- 2" metal putty knife (removing pieces from sanding shims)
- Scissors
- Air compressor (to blow off dust prior to finishing)

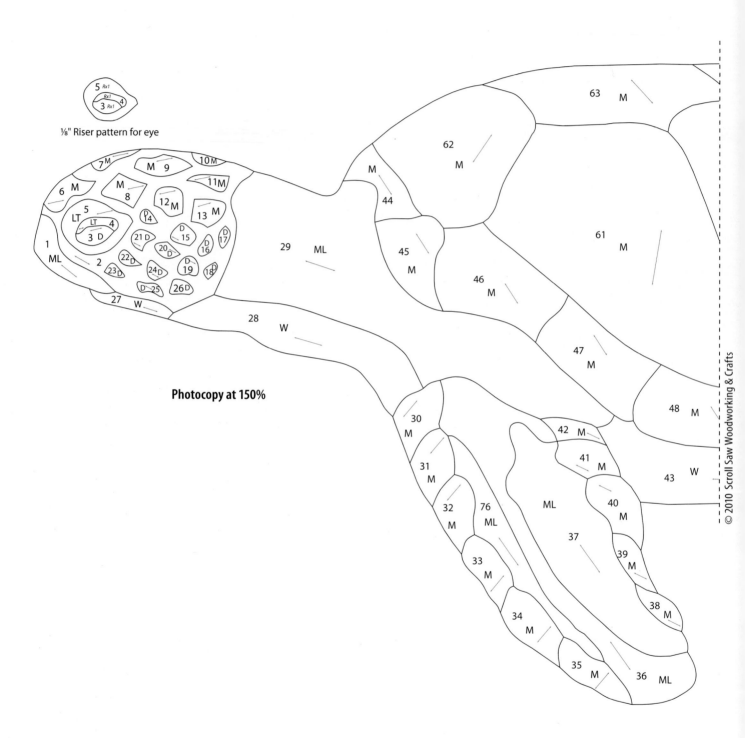

5 Rx1
Rx1
3 Rx1 4

⅛" Riser pattern for eye

7 M
M 9
10 M
6 M
M 8
11 M
5 LT
12 M
LT 4
13 M
3 D
14 D
1
21 D
D 15
D 17
ML
20 D
D 16
2
22 D
23 D
24 D
19 D
18 D
27
D 25
26 D
28 W
W

29 ML

44 M

45 M

46 M

47 M

48 M

30 M

31 M

32 M

33 M

34 M

35 M

36 ML

76 ML

37 ML

40 M

41 M

42 M

43 W

39 M

38 M

62 M

63 M

61 M

Photocopy at 150%

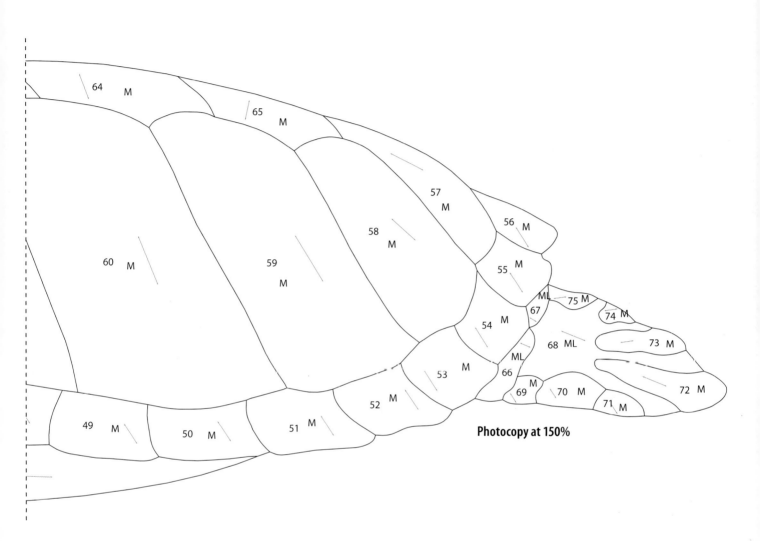

Photocopy at 150%

Pieces #14-#26 may be wood burned to simplify the pattern.

I used lacewood for #1, #29, #36, #37, #66-#68, & #76.

Drill a blade hole for pieces #8, #9, #11-#13 (#14-#26 if desired).

Legend

D - Dark wood shade
M - Medium wood shade
ML - Medium light wood shade
LT - Light wood shade
W - White wood

R - *Raise by ⅛"*

———— Grain direction

On the Ocean Floor

Design by Ellen Brown
Cut by Ben Fink

Tropical fish and marine life are popular decorating motifs for beach houses and bathrooms. This tranquil scene features a school of fish, plant life, coral, and a crab. Frame the fretwork for a quick and easy wall hanging, extend the solid wood at the bottom of the portrait and insert a few hooks for a handy key holder, or use bright acrylic paints to dress up the artwork for display in a child's room.

The design also makes a creative backdrop for your aquarium. I used three panels to dress up a 10-gallon fish tank. You can enlarge

or reduce the pattern, or even alter the dimensions of the border to create a custom backdrop for nearly any size aquarium.

It's easier to stack cut the thin wood and make all the panels you need at the same time. See page 13 for tips on stack cutting techniques. After drilling blade-entry holes and cutting out the fretwork, cut a backing board out of ⅛"-thick plywood, and paint it black. Sand away any rough edges, and glue the panels to the backing board. Apply a clear finish.

Photocopy at 100%

Catch of the Day

By Charles Dearing

This one won't get away! This portrait is the perfect wall hanging for a fishing camp or your den. You could also use the project to embellish a hat or fishing pole rack. Scroll it out of thicker wood (½- to ¾"-thick) and add a few shaker pegs to the bottom, or scroll the design in baltic birch and use it as an insert in your rack.

The pattern is sized to fit in an 8" x 10" frame. For easier cutting, enlarge it 138% for an 11" x 14" frame.

Like most of my designs, I cut this piece out of ¼"-thick plywood. I use spiral blades because they allow me to cut in any direction. Because there are several fragile areas around the mouth of the fish and near the tail, be sure to saturate the pattern with mineral spirits before trying to

remove it. Otherwise, you risk breaking a fragile section when pulling the pattern off. After the mineral spirits dry, sand the piece lightly with 220-grit sandpaper to remove any rough edges left by the spiral blades.

I finish my pieces with several light coats of spray lacquer. For a different look, apply your stain of choice to the plywood, or paint different sections of the backing board different colors—blue for the water, for example.

TIP SAVE YOUR CUTOUTS

Keep the little pieces of wood that you cut out. They will support fragile areas when you sand later.

Photocopy at 100%

Build a Realistic Crab

By Deborah Nicholson

I live on a canal that leads out to the Gulf of Mexico, and the sea creatures in my area are numerous. I find them all interesting, but my favorite is the crab because there are so many different kinds, shapes, and colors. The way the crabs move and pose fascinates me, and I was compelled to capture their likeness in intarsia.

You can create a traditional intarsia crab using 1"-thick wood for all of the pieces. Assemble the crab on a backing board for a flat piece of art. The wire reinforcements used in the legs of the 3-D version are not necessary for a flat crab. Both the flat and 3-D versions make great wall hangings, but the 3-D version is ideal for display on a shelf or end table. Add a few seashells or a decorative net for a fun coastal display.

The body of the 3-D version is created by gluing two 1"-thick pieces of stock together. I glue the blanks for the body before cutting. If your saw is not capable of cutting 2"-thick stock, or you are not comfortable cutting thick wood, cut two body pieces individually and glue them together before shaping. Transfer the pattern using your method of choice. I trace the pattern directly on the stock.

3-D CRAB: CUTTING AND SANDING

1 **Cut and shape the body.** Cut around the perimeter of the body and then cut off the eyes. Shape and round all four sides of the body using a 50-grit sanding belt. The body is thickest in the center and tapers out to the sides. Use the round part of the belt sander to create an indent above the eye area.

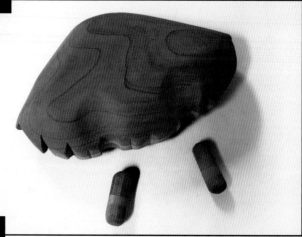

2 **Finish sanding the eyes and body.** Switch to an 80-grit sanding belt to smooth the surface. Round both ends of the eyes. I keep the eyes as long as the body, but you can cut the eye segments to create round eyeballs. Sand everything smooth with a palm sander equipped with 150-grit sandpaper.

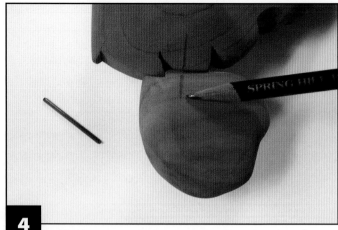

3 **Cut the legs and claws.** Cut one leg at a time and shape the pieces for each leg at the same time. Round them the whole way around. Sand them smooth with finer-grit sandpaper as you did with the body. For the flat intarsia, do not round the bottom of the leg segments where they will be glued to the backing board.

4 **Drill holes to reinforce the legs.** Reinforce the leg joints with a 1¼"-long piece of 14 gauge wire. Drill a ⁵⁄₆₄"-diameter by ⅝"-deep hole where the leg sections join and where the legs meet the body. Draw a pencil line to show the angle of the first hole, and use that line to mark the position of the hole on the next section.

3-D CRAB: ASSEMBLING AND FINISHING

5 **Glue the legs together.** Start with the front legs and work backward, assembling the claws last. Prop the body up on scrap wood to create the desired pose. Apply glue to each wire and slide the pieces into place. The end of each leg should touch the ground. Allow the glue to dry after each leg is assembled.

6 **Finish the crabs.** Reinforce the joints with a few drops of glue. Paint the eyes and claws with black acrylic paint and glue them in place. If you cut the crab from pine, add some extra color with a wash of burnt sienna acrylic paint followed by a wash of red acrylic paint. Apply a clear spray finish to seal the project.

Materials & Tools

Materials:
- 1" x 10" x 12" red cedar or wood of choice (flat crab)
- ¼" x 10" x 12" hardboard (backing board for flat crab)
- 1" x 10" x 18" red cedar or wood of choice (3-D crab)
- 14-gauge wire (3-D crab)
- Acrylic paint: black, burnt sienna, red
- Clear spray finish
- Assorted grits of sandpaper
- 50-grit & 80-grit sanding belt
- Wood glue

Tools:
- #5 reverse-tooth blades or blades of choice
- Drill with ⁵⁄₆₄"-diameter drill bit
- Belt sander, palm sander, or sanding tools of choice

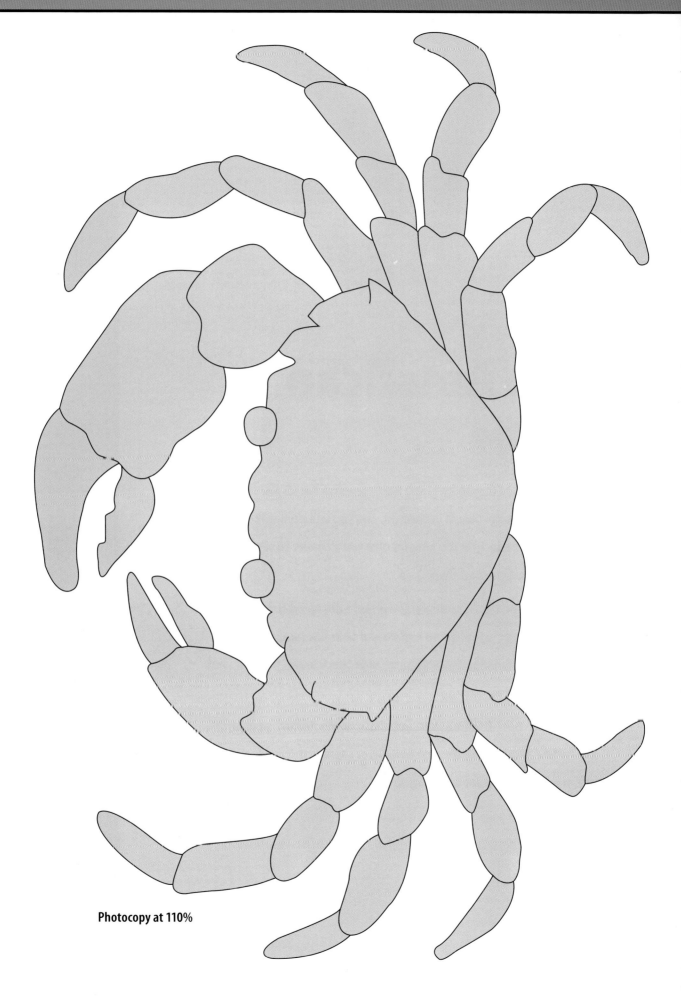

Photocopy at 110%

North American Wildlife

Some animals just inspire awe, and North America has its fair share of those. Elk, bear, deer, wolf—say it in the wild, and you will probably see heads swivel. The 10 projects in this chapter give you a chance to capture that wonder in your own workshop.

On the large end of the animal scale, there are an intarsia elk portrait, a moose-themed coat rack, and buffalo and bear layerscapes. Filling out the powerful category are a wolf trivet, wolf "pack mate" portrait, and grizzly bear portrait.

If you like deer, feel free to try your hand at the lighted woodland shadowbox and a trophy display shelf. Or, to capture the peace of a secluded lake, have a go at the loons fretwork.

Whether you keep your handiwork or give it away, these trophies will be a welcome reminder of the majesty of nature and its creatures.

Lighted Woodland Shadowbox, page 79

Howling Wolf Trivet

By Theresa & Emily Ekdom

Inlay and relief-cutting techniques can be intimidating, especially for a beginner, but this design makes it easy to learn the basics. Once you know the technique, experiment with alternate uses. Use the design to create a box lid, or reduce the pattern for use as a magnet.

My daughter drew this design when she was 15 for a 5" x 5" wooden quilt square. I fell in love with the design and enlarged it for use as a trivet or plaque.

Pay attention to the color and grain direction of the wood. I use red cedar with white streaks to simulate clouds in the evening sky. The grain lines in the cherry give the look of windblown terrain. Make three copies of the pattern to use when cutting the project.

Step 1: **Determine the table angle.** Make a few test cuts to find the right angle for cutting the inlays. Tilt the right side of the saw table down 3 ½°. Stack two pieces of scrap from the wood you plan to use for the inlay. Cut a circle counterclockwise with a #3 blade. Separate the stack. Place the top piece of wood into the hole in the bottom piece. It should fit flush. If the inlay sticks out, increase the angle of the table tilt. If the inlay sinks into the hole, reduce the angle of the table tilt. Continue to adjust the angle of the table and cut test inlays until you are satisfied with the fit. Note the angle of the table.

Step 2: **Inlay the moon.** Use hot glue to stack together the red cedar and the aspen. Attach a copy of the pattern to the aspen. Drill a blade-entry hole where indicated on the pattern. This area will be removed when the horizon is cut, so the size of the hole is not important. Cut counterclockwise around the moon. Separate the stack, remove the pattern, and glue the moon into the sky. Sand the back of the piece flat.

Step 3: **Cut the horizon.** Return the table to square and attach the cherry to the top of the aspen/red cedar with hot glue. Attach a copy of the pattern to the cherry. Cut along the horizon line, remove the pattern, and edge glue the cherry to the aspen and red cedar.

Step 4: **Cut the wolf.** Reset the table to the proper angle determined in step 1. Use hot glue to stack the piece of walnut on top of the background stock created in step 3. Adhere the pattern to the walnut. Drill a blade-entry hole at the top of the hind foot and in the middle of the eye line with a ¹⁄₃₂"-diameter bit. Start at the hind foot and cut counterclockwise around the perimeter of the wolf, including the detail lines. Return the table to square and cut along the eye line. Glue the wolf into the background. Sand the front and back of the inlay.

Step 5: **Complete the trivet.** Glue and clamp the inlay onto a ½"-thick backing board. When dry, sand the edges to ensure a smooth surface. Drill ⅜"-diameter holes in each corner of the backing piece. Be careful not to drill through into the inlay stock. Glue the hardwood plugs in place. Apply a coat of tung oil or your finish of choice.

Photocopy at 100%

Materials & Tools

Materials:

- ¼" x 7" x 7" red cedar or red wood of choice (sky)
- ¼" x 7" x 7" aspen or white wood of choice (moon)
- ¼" x 7" x 7" cherry or medium brown wood of choice (ground)
- ¼" x 7" x 7" walnut or dark wood of choice (wolf)
- ½" x 7" x 7" pine (backing board)

(Note: Advanced scrollers can use smaller pieces of wood by carefully aligning the patterns and the wood when creating the stacks.)

- 4 each hardwood plugs with ⅜"-diameter shaft
- Wood glue
- Tung oil or finish of choice
- Assorted grits of sandpaper

Tools:

- #3 reverse-tooth blades or blades of choice
- Drill with assorted drill bits
- Hot glue gun with glue sticks
- Clamps of choice

Hardwood plugs mounted to the reverse side serve as feet for the trivet.

Majestic Elk

By Kathy Wise

This majestic portrait of a bull elk will be admired by hunters and wildlife enthusiasts alike. In addition to creating the design as a wall hanging, you can easily use it as an overlay for a gun cabinet or alter the base to accommodate Shaker pegs and use it as a coat rack.

This piece was inspired by a family trip to northern Michigan. We visited a rural area near Atlanta, MI, where elk were relocated many years ago. We watched as a large bull elk sprinted across a field and stopped near the gravel road where we were parked in our car. He lifted his head to test the air, then crossed the road like he owned it. We were thankful to have been at the right place at the right time to see such an awesome creature.

Shaping individual tufts of fur adds depth and dimension.

Materials & Tools

Materials:
- 1" x 6" x 7" white wood such as poplar
- 1"x 8" x 13" light-colored wood such as light sycamore
- 1"x 8" x 10" medium-light wood such as medium-light sycamore
- 1" x 8" x 13" light colored wood such as ash
- 1" x 6" x 6" medium-colored wood such as beech
- 1" x 8" x 20" medium-dark wood such as black walnut
- 1" x 8" x 18" dark wood such as wenge
- ¾" x 6" x 22" medium-black wood such as bocote
- ¾" x 6" x 22" dark wood such as wenge
- ¼" x 19" x 26" plywood or Masonite (backer)
- Wood glue
- Cyanoacrylate (CA) glue
- Spray varnish or finish of choice

Tools:
- #5 reverse-tooth blades or blades of choice
- Pneumatic drum sander or sander of choice

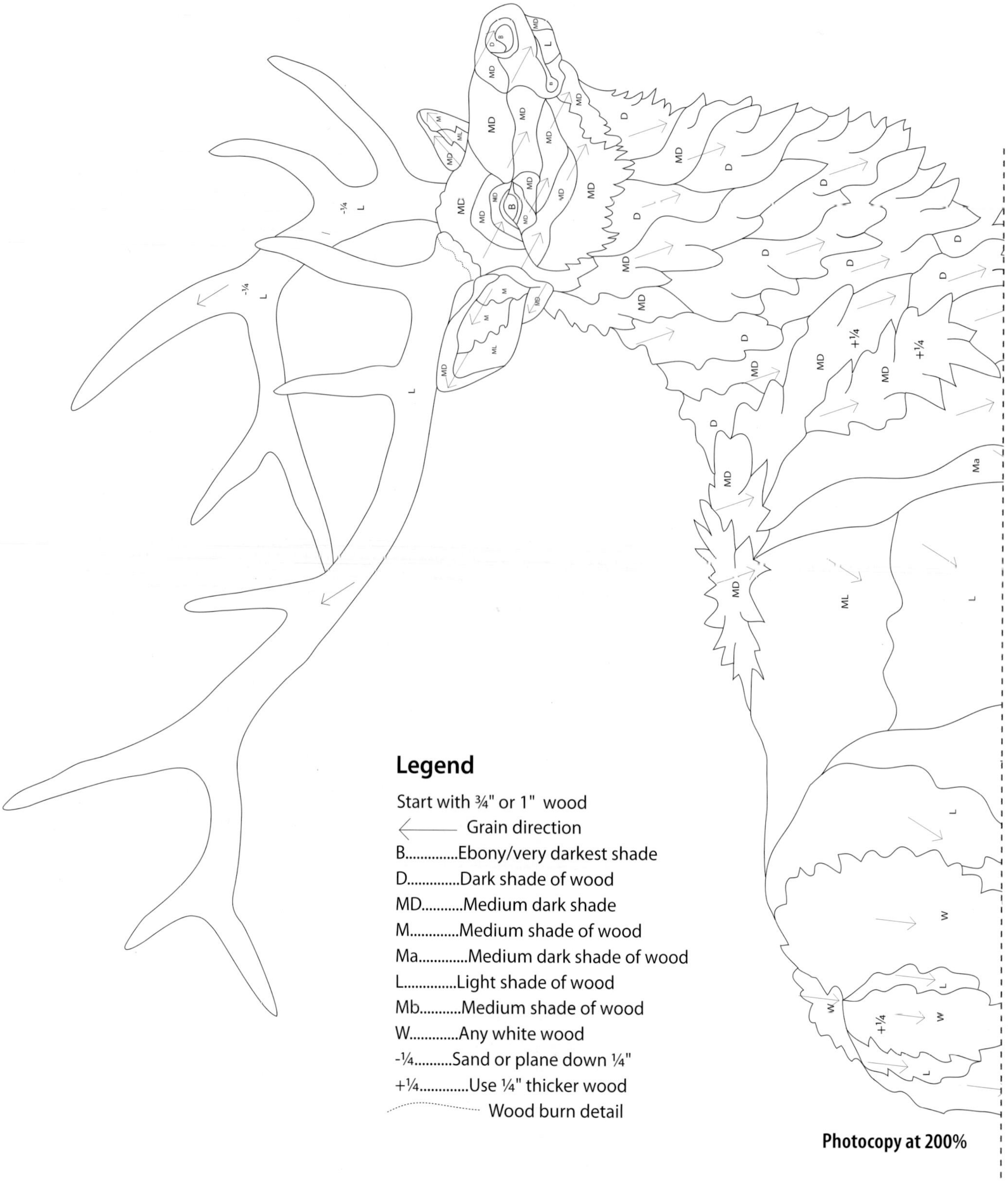

Legend

Start with ¾" or 1" wood

⟵   Grain direction

B.............Ebony/very darkest shade

D.............Dark shade of wood

MD..........Medium dark shade

M............Medium shade of wood

Ma............Medium dark shade of wood

L............Light shade of wood

Mb..........Medium shade of wood

W............Any white wood

-¼..........Sand or plane down ¼"

+¼.............Use ¼" thicker wood

················· Wood burn detail

Photocopy at 200%

Photocopy at 200%

Wood burn hair
detail if desired

Buffalo Layerscape

Designed by Lora S. Irish

I spend a lot of time sketching and drawing wildlife scenes. When I was challenged to convert the scenes into a layered scroll saw pattern, I eagerly accepted. Separating the individual elements into layers adds tremendous depth and contrast to the portrait. I can break down the background, main subject, and foreground into individual layers or use the layers to create shadows and depth. The layers are easy to scroll individually. When assembled, they create a complex finished look.

Assembly view

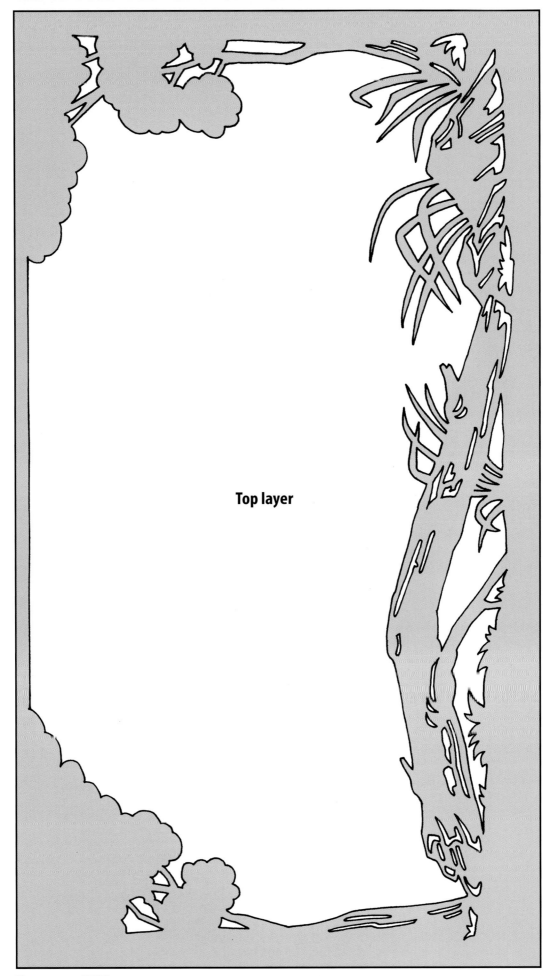

Top layer

Photocopy at 150%

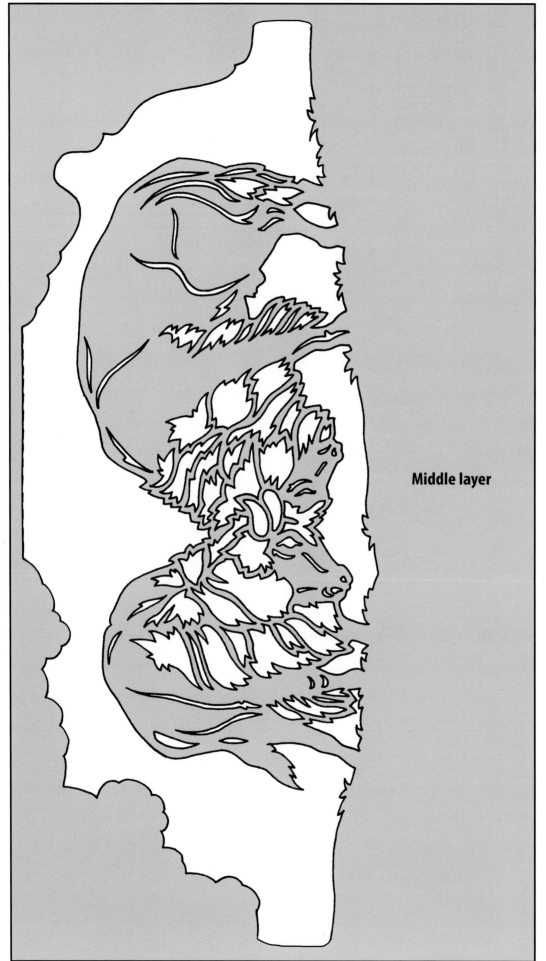

Middle layer

Photocopy at 150%

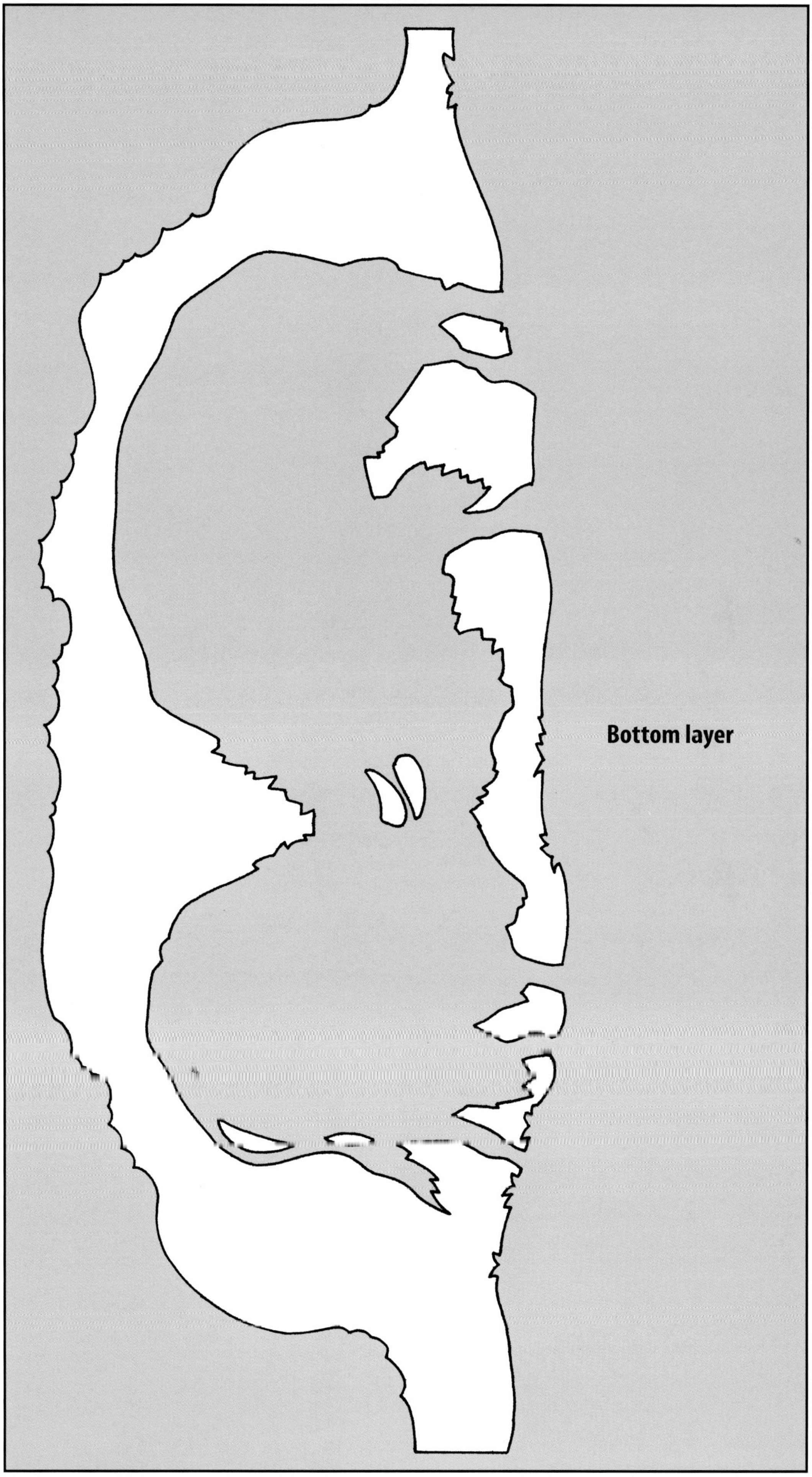

Bottom layer

Photocopy at 150%

Bear Layerscape

Designed by Lora S. Irish

Assembly view

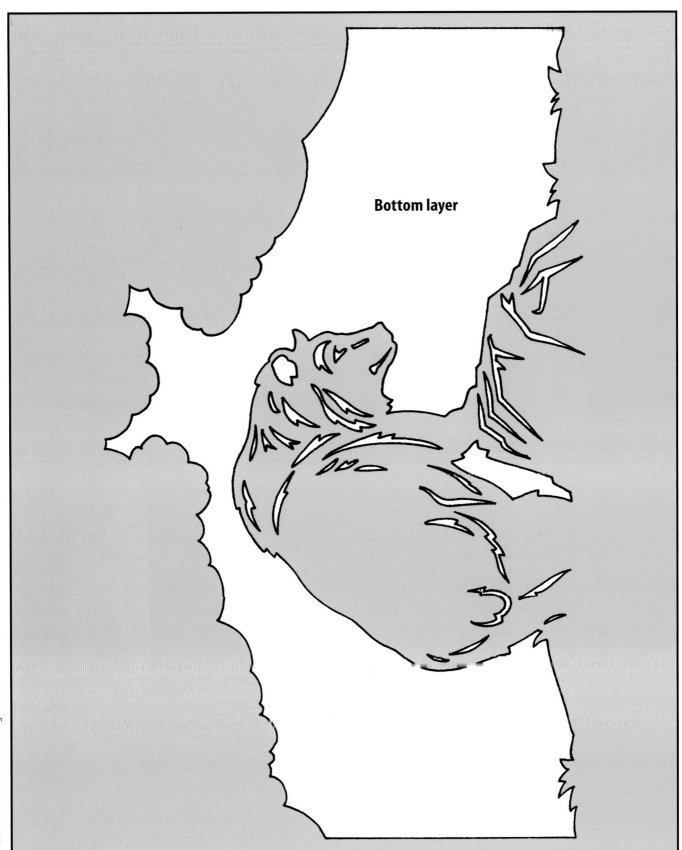

Bottom layer

Photocopy at 105%

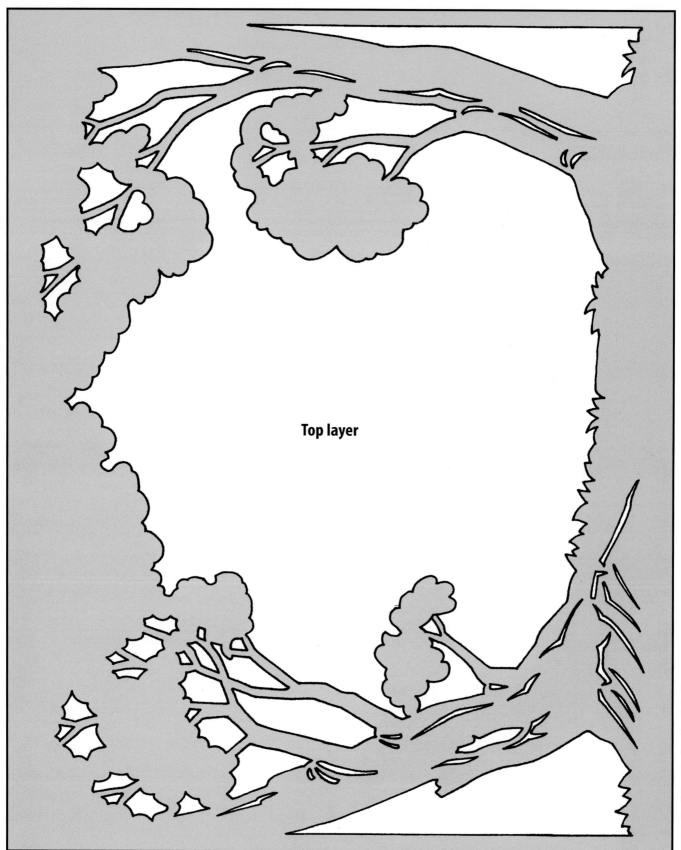

Top layer

Photocopy at 105%

Lighted Woodland Shadowbox

By Tom Sevy
Designed by Volker Arnold

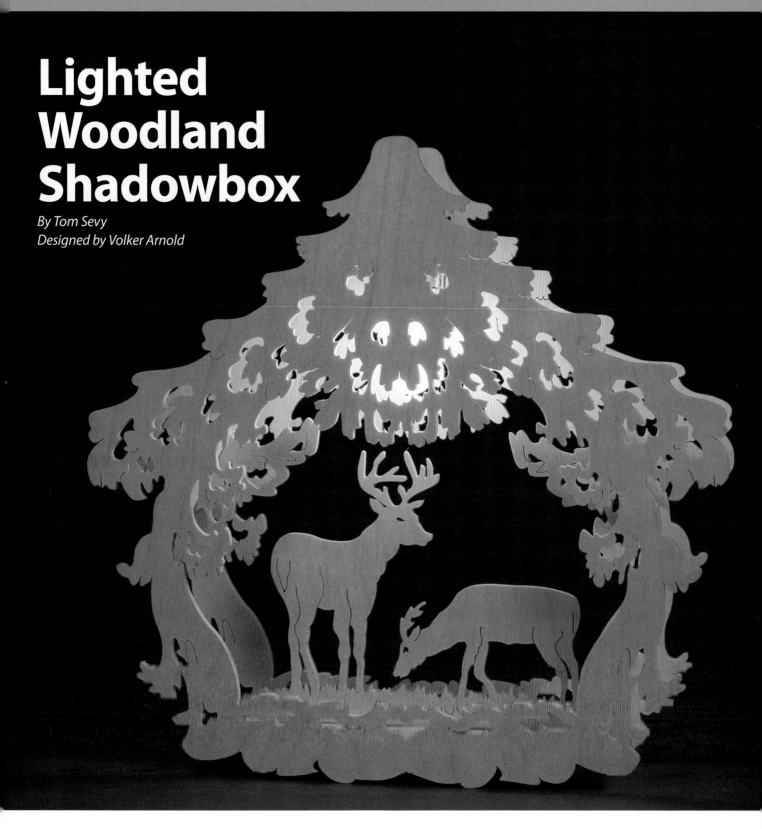

This charming night light is easy to assemble and is sure to be a hit with hunters and wildlife lovers. It looks great hanging in a window or casting a soft glow from a table or a child's dresser.

The traditional German method of display is to insert a light in the top and hang in a window. You can use an electric or battery-operated light or display the project without any light source.

Photocopy at 100%

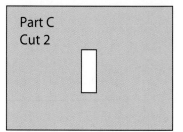

Part C
Cut 2

Part B
Cut 1

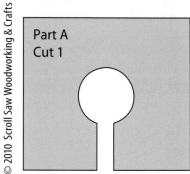

Part A
Cut 1

Photocopy at 100%

Step 1: Stack cut the trees, small tree branches, and side spacers. Cut only a single layer for the deer, lamp-holding piece, and bottom spacer.

Step 2: The easiest way to cut the 1"-diameter hole for the light is to use a Forstner bit. Drill the hole before cutting the lamp-holding piece to size so you have something to hold on to. You could also cut the hole with your scroll saw.

Step 3: Assemble the project. Use cyanoacrylate glue to glue the branches (Part D) to the side spacers (Part C). Glue the three spacers (Parts B & C) and the lamp-holding piece (Part A) to one of the sides according to the dashed lines on the pattern. Make sure that each one is at a right angle to the side piece. Glue the other side piece in place, making sure both side pieces are aligned with each other. Finally, glue the deer in place.

Step 4: If applying a finish, assemble the project before application to ensure a stronger glue bond. In Germany it is traditional to leave scrolled decorations unfinished for a lighter wood color.

Materials & Tools

Materials:
- 2 each ⅛" x 9½" x 9½" Baltic birch (front, back and branches)
- ⅛" x 4½" x 6" Baltic birch (deer insert)
- ⅛" x 2" x 9½" (spacers)
- Light assembly (optional)

Tools:
- #1 reverse-tooth blades or blades of choice
- Cyanoacrylate glue or glue of choice

SPECIAL SOURCES:
Light sets are available from National Artcraft: 888-937-2723, www.nationalartcraft.com

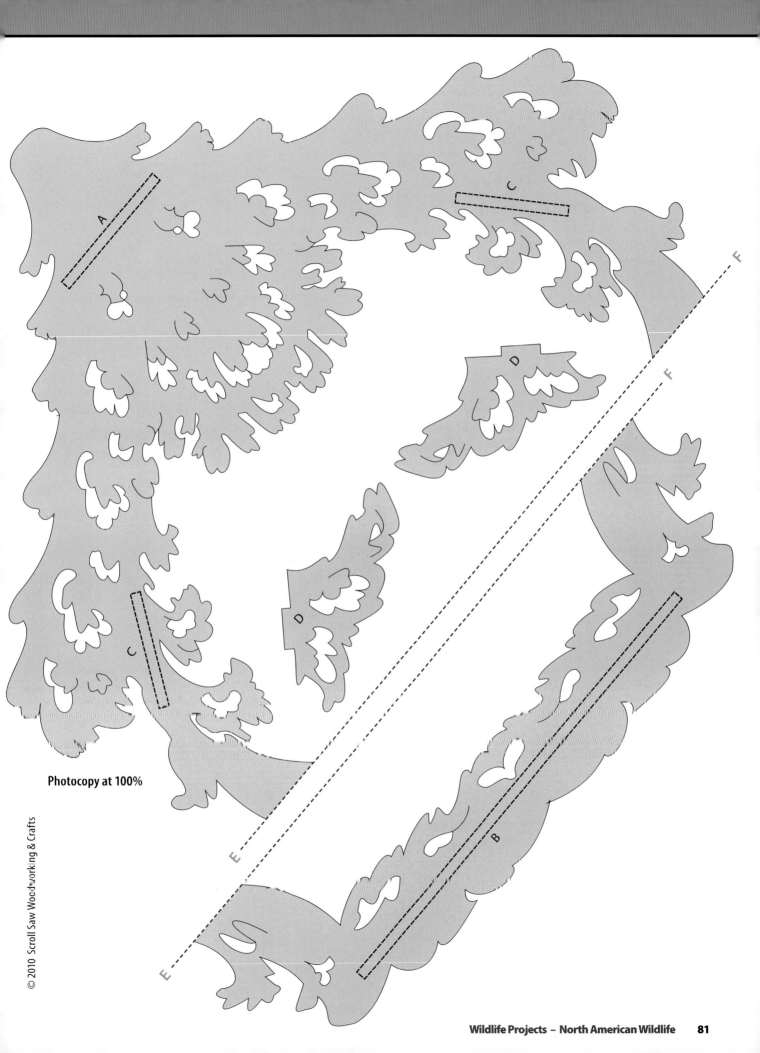

Photocopy at 100%

Pack Mates

By Kevin Daly

This image captures the beauty and majesty of two wolf "brothers." The design is one of my personal favorites. Wolves are a popular subject, and I sell a lot of portraits based on these noble and often misunderstood creatures.

I knew that a slab of spalted mahogany I had on my shelf was the perfect medium for this design. Mahogany cuts well and resists breaking in fragile areas. Ash and maple are other woods I've had good luck with.

Cutting hardwood slabs requires you to cut more slowly and use more caution when working in delicate areas. The thin areas are prone to snapping along the grain lines. I use ⅜"-thick or thicker stock and a #1 reverse, skip-tooth flat blade.

This pattern contains about 500 cuts. Cut the branch and wolf details before cutting the large open areas. I drill blade-entry holes in groups of 50; this allows me to cut for about 45 minutes and get up to stretch a bit while I drill the next group.

To finish the portrait, apply Danish oil and several coats of clear spray lacquer. Attach your backing of choice; I use black felt glued to the back of the portrait with tacky glue.

Materials & Tools

Materials:
- ⅜" x 11" x 14" mahogany or wood of choice
- Danish oil
- Semi-gloss spray lacquer or finish of choice
- Sandpaper, assorted grits
- Tacky glue
- Black felt

Tools:
- Drill with #63 drill bit
- #1 reverse, skip-tooth blades or blades of choice

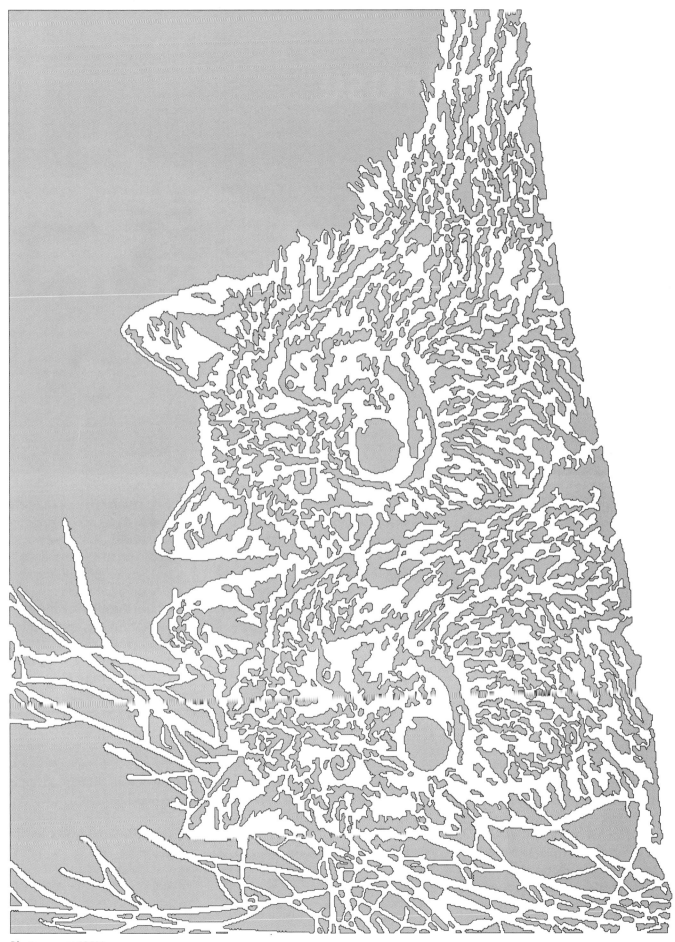

Photocopy at 135%

Majestic Moose Coat Rack

By Terry Foltz

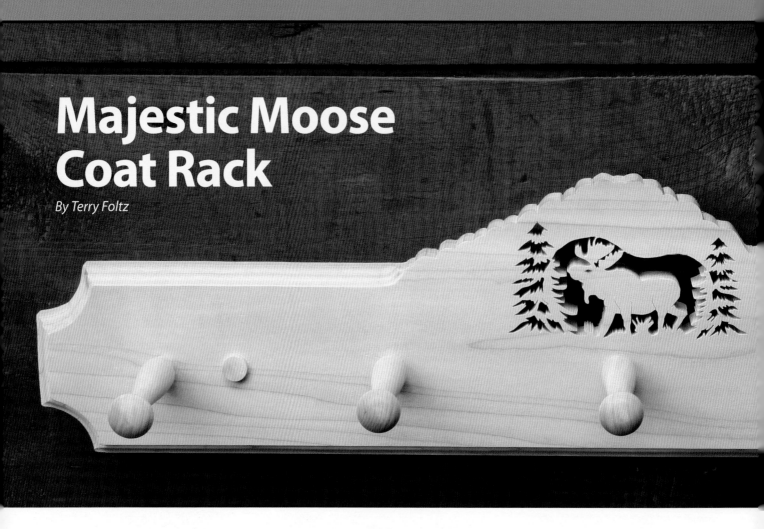

Whether you're looking for a functional piece for your hunting cabin or a rustic home accent, this striking moose scene is sure to spice up your entry way. Simple construction techniques make it a perfect weekend project. Try scrolling a different scene onto the rack for an endless variety of projects to suit any taste. The scenic moose pattern can also be used to embellish any number of items or as a stand-alone project.

Step 1:   Select your wood. I try to use rough-cut lumber; it gives the project a more rustic feel. It is possible to use a board straight from the store. I usually use cedar or pine for my coat racks. Run the board through the planer a couple times or sand it smooth with 150-grit sandpaper. Use progressively finer grits of sandpaper up through 320-grit.

Step 2:   Apply the pattern to the wood. In order to make sure my pattern is in the exact position I want it, I tape it in place first. Position the pattern where you want it, and put a piece of tape in the middle of the top and bottom of the pattern. Remove one piece of tape, fold the pattern back, and apply rubber cement to that half. When you've positioned that half, remove the other piece of tape, fold that half back, apply the rubber cement, and secure it to the wood.

Step 3:   Cut the outline of your coat rack. Use your blade of choice—I prefer thinner blades such as a #2/0 or #3/0 reverse-tooth blade.

Step 4:   Drill the blade-entry holes. Use a 1/32"-diameter drill bit in a drill press, if possible. The largest bit you should use is a 1/16"-diameter bit.

Step 5:   Bevel the sides of the coat rack. If you are making the traditional rack, use a router with a beading bit to round over the edges. Use caution with the router—practice on scrap wood until you don't burn the wood or tear out the edges. You can also lightly round over the corners with sandpaper.

Step 6:   Insert the blade through the blade-entry hole. I use a #2/0 blade with 27 teeth per inch. These blades give me the sharpest corners. Start by cutting the trees. Then cut out the grass and moose's legs. Cut out the outline of the moose. Finally cut the background.

Step 7:   Drill the holes for the shaker pegs. I use 1/2"-diameter pegs, so I drill 1/2"-diameter holes 11/16"-deep—slightly deeper than the peg's post. Test fit the pegs to make sure they sit flush against the rack.

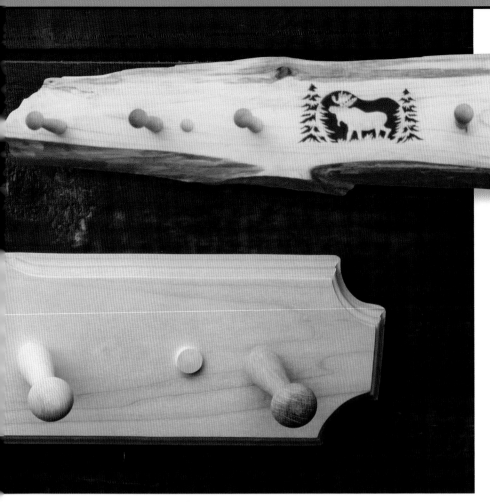

Bring the wilderness inside with this handy coat rack that can be as rustic— or as finished—as you want.

Materials & Tools

Materials:
- ¾" x 8" x 24" cedar, pine, or wood of choice
- Sandpaper, 150, 220, 320-grits
- Transparent tape
- Rubber cement
- Linseed oil or finish of choice
- 5 each ½"-diameter x 3½"-long Shaker pegs
- 2 each ½"-diameter screw hole buttons
- Wood glue

Tools:
- Planer (optional)
- #2/0 single skip-tooth blades, #2/0, or #3/0 ultra-premium reverse-tooth blades, or blades of choice
- Drill or drill press
- ¹⁄₃₂", ¼"-, and ½"-diameter drill bits
- Orbital sander or sanding block
- #6 round artist's brush
- Brush of choice to apply finish
- Router with ⅝"-diameter beading bit (optional)
- Hammer

You may need to sand the pegs down a little bit until they fit in the holes.

Step 8: Drill the screw holes.
Set your drill to go about halfway through the wood, and drill a countersinking hole based on the size of your screw-cover buttons. Then drill a ¼"-diameter hole through the board where indicated on the pattern. The screw holes are set up based on the standard 16"-centers used in frame building— you may need to adjust the placement of your holes based on where the coat rack will be located.

Step 9: Remove the pattern and any remaining adhesive.
Then sand the project with 220-grit sandpaper and 320-grit sandpaper.

Step 10: Glue the pegs in place.
Apply a little glue to the posts of each peg, and push it as far as possible into the holes. Place the coat rack on the floor, and place a piece of scrap wood on top of the pegs. Hammer the scrap wood lightly until the pegs are firmly seated against the rack. Press the screw buttons in place while you finish the rack—do not glue them in place.

Step 11: Finish the coat rack.
Sign and date the rack. Remove all the dust with a rag and blow out any dust that accumulated on the design. Apply your finish of choice. I use Tried and True linseed oil, but you can use your natural-colored finish of choice. Use a #6 large artist's round brush to apply the finish to the moose design. You can use a larger brush on the other areas. Apply two coats of oil, and allow the piece to dry totally before hanging it on the wall.

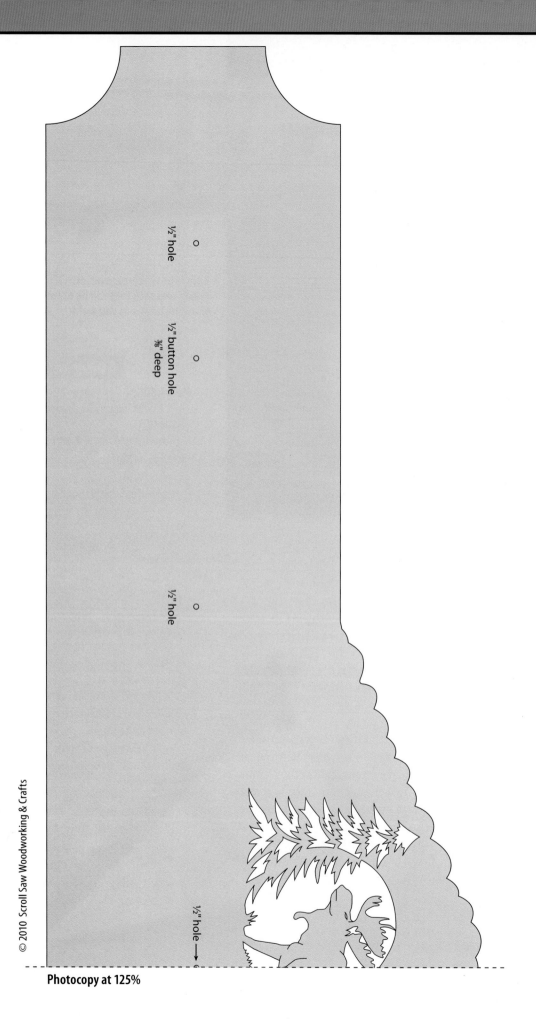

½" hole

½" button hole
⅜" deep

½" hole

½" hole

Photocopy at 125%

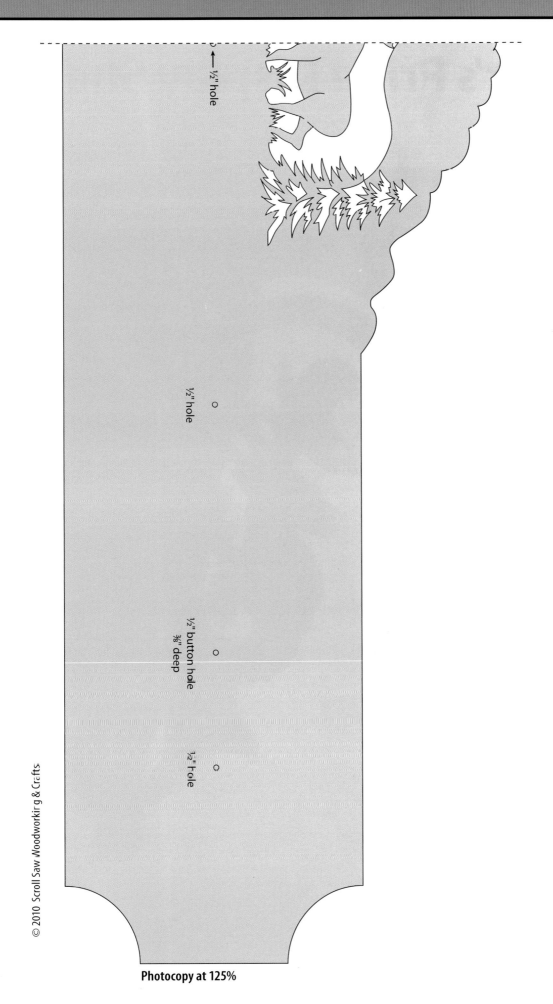

½" hole

½" hole

½" button hole
⅜" deep

½" hole

Photocopy at 125%

Hunter's Pride Display Shelf

By John A. Nelson

Cut by Michael Jamgochian

This fretwork shelf combines a masculine theme with the attractive, flowing lines of traditional fretwork. The easy-to-assemble project produces a functional shelf to display memorabilia or a prized hunting photo.

This shelf was cut from Baltic birch plywood and finished with an elm stain. You can stack cut the individual pieces to produce a perfectly matched set. After cutting the fretwork, remove any rough areas with sandpaper. Stain the wood if desired and use your glue of choice to assemble the shelf. I use cyanoacrylate (CA) glue and apply a couple coats of spray lacquer to disguise any glue that squeezes out.

Materials & Tools

Materials:
- ¼" x 10½" x 12¼" hardwood or wood of choice (back)
- ¼" x 7" x 13" hardwood or wood of choice (shelf)
- ¼" x 6" x 10½" hardwood or wood of choice (shelf support)
- Stain (optional)
- Cyanoacrylate (CA) glue
- Assorted grits of sandpaper
- Finish of choice

Tools:
- #3 reverse-tooth blades or blades of choice
- Drill with ¹⁄₁₆"-diameter drill bit
- Brushes to apply finish (optional)

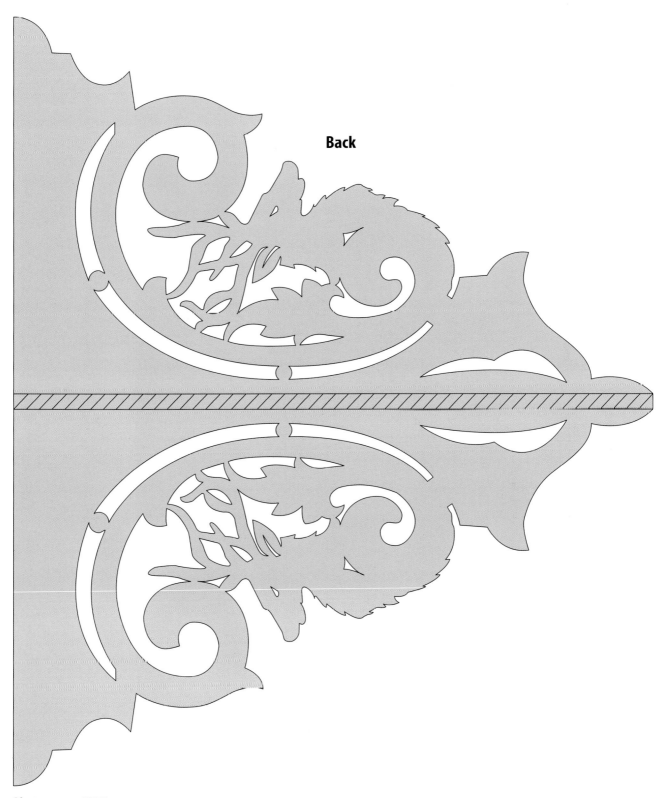

Back

Photocopy at 150%

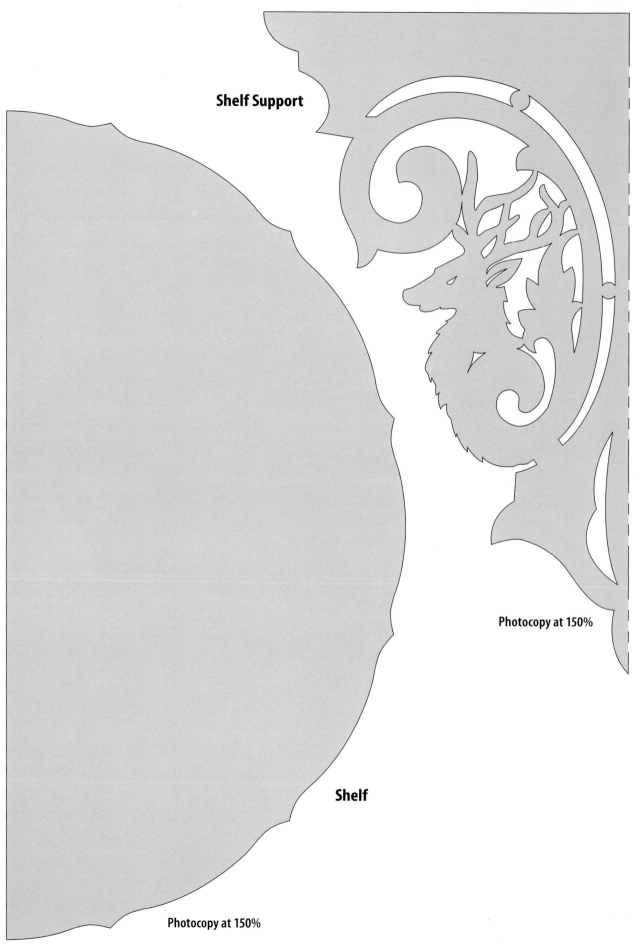

Shelf Support

Photocopy at 150%

Shelf

Photocopy at 150%

Grizzly Bear

By Gary Browning

Capture the majesty of the grizzly bear in this large portrait project. If you are new to making portraits on your scroll saw, use this walk-through to help you learn some of the basic techniques. Those not-so-new to portrait making will take away not only a bear portrait to keep or to give, but also tips for making their next projects.

Step 1: Prepping and adhering the pattern. Select your project size and photocopy the pattern accordingly. Once you cut your wood blank to size, transfer the pattern onto the wood.

It's distracting when the pattern lifts up or tears, especially on tight cuts, so I cover the entire wood cutting surface with painter's tape. Usually blue, it leaves little to no residue when removed. Spray the back of your pattern and the surface of the painter's tape with a heavy coat of temporary bond spray adhesive. Place the pattern on the top of the painter's tape right away for a good solid bond. Once you've finished cutting, the tape peels off easily. If I'm stack cutting, I simply place a few wood blanks under the top piece and tape the surface of the cutting area with

2" clear packaging tape. I wrap about 2" around the back side. The packaging tape sticks well, holds a stack together, and helps lubricate the blade while cutting.

Step 2: Making blade-entry holes. Drill your blade-entry holes in each cut-out section of the pattern using a #61 bit.

Choose as large a bit as you can to drill blade-entry holes. A larger-than-normal hole makes blade changes easier, especially when you are steadying your project with one hand.

Step 3:   **Cutting the pattern.**
Begin to cut out the pattern using a #⅖ spiral blade, a #2 reverse standard blade, or your blade of choice. Start from the center of the pattern and work out to the four edges of the pattern. After each cut, move to the piece closest to the one you just cut out.

If you are cutting a larger piece, such as 16" x 20", it helps to stack cut two pieces at once for more support, especially if you are using plywood. Stack cutting helps support the fragile pieces and yields a second project without dramatically slowing down the rate you feed wood into the blade. If you need to cut two of the piece, it also cuts saw time in half.

Large projects generate a lot of dust, so it's a good idea to stop once in a while and vacuum. Otherwise, especially if your shop area is not well ventilated, you may be breathing more dust than you would like to.

If the pattern is larger than your saw's throat depth, try a spiral blade. With teeth on all sides, spiral blades give you greater flexibility than regular blades and can dart in and out of tight spaces. This flexibility makes it easier to cut larger projects because you don't have to move the wood around the blade.

After cutting a large inside section, it may be helpful to keep the waste wood inside the project,

using clear packaging tape to hold it in place. This technique will help to minimize the stress on the fragile pieces, especially if you flex the wood while threading a blade. If you do make a mistake and a small piece breaks off, don't panic. Glue it back on after the cutting is complete, or smooth the break point with your scroll saw.

Step 4:   **Removing the burrs.**
Once all of the cutting is done, remove the tape. On the back side of the portrait, remove any burrs of wood caused by the blade.

I use a rotary tool with a small drum sander attachment, held at an angle to the wood, and lightly go over each cut-out area. Wear safety goggles and a dust mask if you try this technique.

Step 5:   **Sanding the project.**
With a palm sander, lightly sand the front surface of the wood with a few grades of sandpaper.

Because the weight of the palm sander is distributed, it does not tend to break the fragile pieces of the project. Just be sure that you don't push down with too much pressure. Usually the weight of the sander itself is enough pressure. I start with 150-grit sandpaper and finish with 220.

Step 6:   **Applying a protective finish.** I suggest a clear finish, which will help protect it from the sun and, with a dark background, gives the portrait dimension. Staining the wood too dark will diminish that effect.

Another option is to leave it unfinished.

If you choose the clear finish, spray a light coat over the portrait and let it dry. Then spray on additional coats if desired.

Step 7:   **Framing the piece.**
Hot-glue the background felt or material to the back side of the

wood, and put the portrait in a frame behind glass.

With light wood, a dark background adds dimension. I recommend a black frame for the same reason, especially if your project is large and you cannot mat it in black. You may also want to try using a dark background, light-colored wood for the portrait, a black mat, and a light-colored frame.

If you use ¼" stock and the wood bulges out from behind the frame a bit, try installing a wire hanger and two self-adhesive cushioning tabs on the bottom two corners of the back of the frame, opposite the wire hanger. This will lift the frame away from the wall slightly to make room for the bulge.

Don't forget to sign your piece of art and show it off to your friends and family.

Materials & Tools

Materials:
- ¼" x 11" x 14" Baltic birch or oak plywood
- Sandpaper, course, medium, and fine grits
- 11" x 14" frame (or custom frame)
- 2" clear packaging tape
- Painter's tape
- Temporary bond spray adhesive
- Clear coat finish spray
- Black felt or dark background material

Tools:
- #2/0 spiral blade, #2 reverse standard, or blade of choice
- Drill with #61 bit or a bit that is smaller than the cutout areas
- Palm sander (optional)
- Hot-glue gun
- Rotary tool with mini drum sander bit

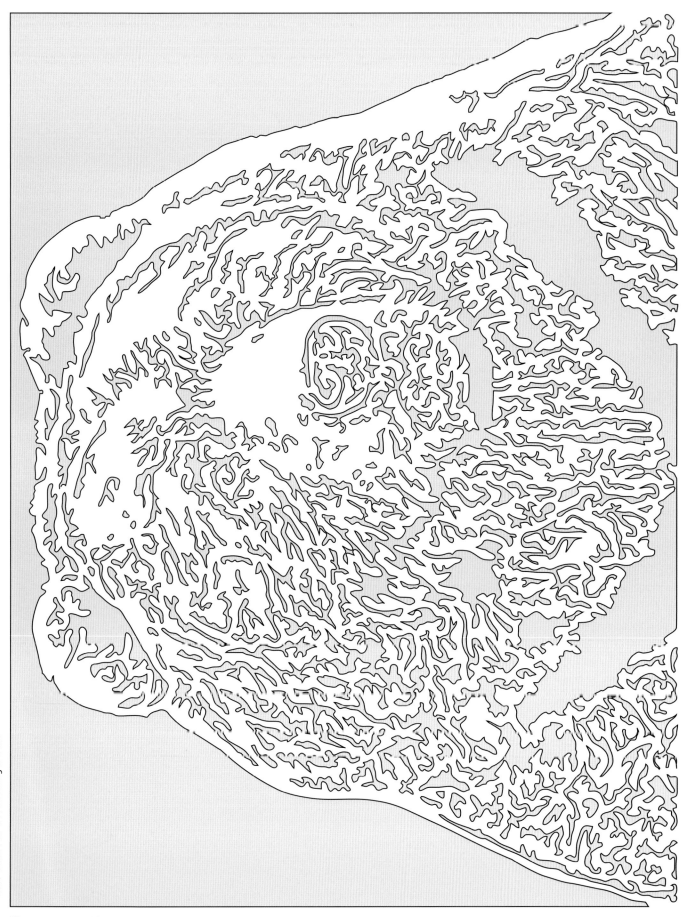

Photocopy at 150%

Loons

Designed by Ellen Brown

The loons remind me of a peaceful day at the lake. The design is a great way to embellish a cabinet in a hunting cabin—or the back of a shotgun rack.

Another option would be to cut it out of a thicker piece of wood and turn it into a trivet.

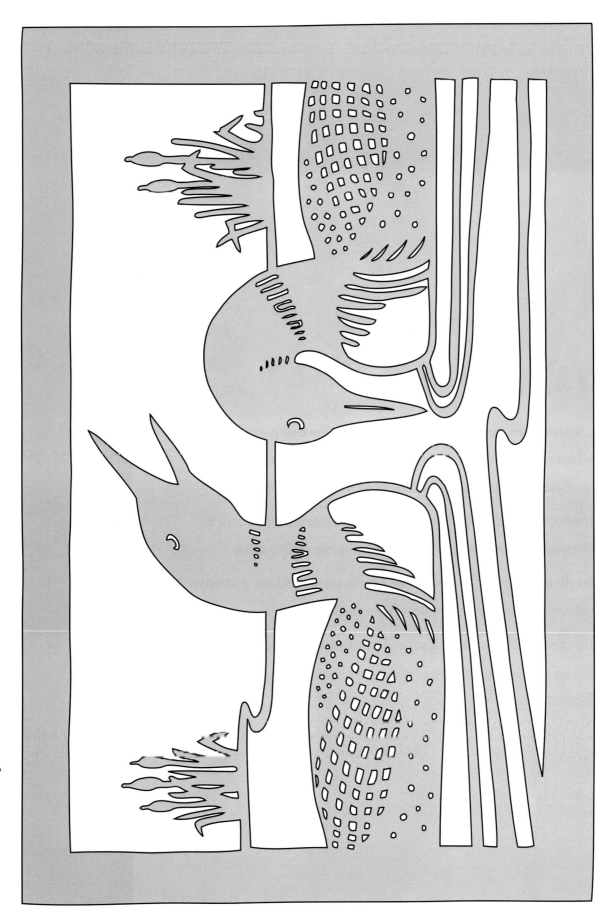

Photocopy at 100%

Big Cats

Lion, leopard, tiger, cheetah, jaguar—these aren't the kind of big cats you're likely to see hunting nearby. But with a little time and skill, the five projects in this chapter can help you create wooden versions to grace your home.

The lion is an ideal subject for segmented portraiture; it brings such life to his impressive mane that you may just imagine him roaring at you.

For the leopard, tiger, and jaguar, we have detailed individual portraits that underscore the power and grace of these well-known predators.

The cheetah is known for its spots and its speed, but this portrait focuses on a softer side of its personality as three young cubs nestle close to their mother.

Tiger Portrait, page 106

Roaring Lion Segmentation

By Neal Moore

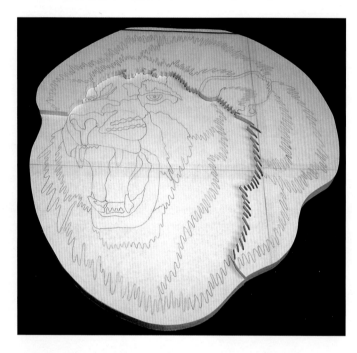

When I first started cutting segmented portraiture, I fell in love with the simplicity of the technique and the amazing results that could be achieved.

Although the finished Roaring Lion portrait looks impressive, it is not a difficult project. I recommend that you read through the steps and refer to the photos before starting. I use ½" poplar and a #3 reverse-tooth blade. The finished image measures 14" x 12". You may need to edge-glue two or more boards together to get the width you need.

Cutting the Segments

Step 1: Use scissors to trim around the pattern, leaving a ½" margin outside the lines. Attach the pattern with the grain oriented top to bottom.

Step 2: Remove the waste wood from around the pattern. Cut around the margin you left on the pattern.

Step 3: Divide the pattern into sections. Locate the pattern line that runs through the lion's head from left to right. Cut on that line as shown, dividing the project into two pieces.

Step 4: Divide the two sections into smaller sections. On the smaller piece, cut the pattern line that runs around the top of the lion's ear and exit the cut through the waste of the margin.

Step 5: Cut the line that runs around the bottom of the lion's ear. This will allow you to remove the whole ear as one piece. Now the lion's head is divided into four pieces. Place the three smaller pieces aside, and move on to the largest piece.

Step 6: Drill blade-entry holes for the lion's left eye and lower teeth. You will need only two holes. Drill the hole for the eye just inside, and touching, the pattern line for the inner part of the eye. Cut and remove the inner part of the eye first. Then cut the outer part. Thread the blade through the other hole, and cut the small teeth from the lower part of the lion's mouth.

Step 7: Cut out the rest of the segments. When done, assemble the segments on your work table. It's a good practice to assemble the segments at your work table as you cut. Remove the patterns. At the same time, remove any burrs left by the cutting. Stain each individual piece according to the staining guide and the instructions provided before gluing up your project.

Staining

I prepare my work table for staining by taping down a sheet of waxed butcher's paper, wax side up. I then tape a few layers of paper towels over that to create an absorbent surface for the segments to dry on. When finished, I fold it all to the center and discard the whole thing.

To stain, just dip the segment in the stain, slosh it around, and place it aside to dry.

I devised a paint-by-numbers approach to staining. Study the staining chart on the next page before you begin. It may be helpful to note the stain to be used on the back of each piece. Refer to the color-coded staining chart and the reference photo often during the staining process. Remove the segments, one at a time, from the assembled cutout, and stain them accordingly.

Staining Key:

☐	No stain, pieces remain white.
☐	Slosh the pieces in golden oak, and wipe off most of the stain. This gives a very light color to the wood.
☐	Slosh the pieces in golden oak, and do not wipe the stain off.
☐	Stain with golden oak and "smear mix" with dark walnut. This is done by first sloshing the segment in golden oak stain. Then, while the golden oak is still wet, use a small brush, and smear a little dark walnut stain where needed to approximate the color as shown in the reference photo. Use a very small amount of dark walnut at first, and add more as you feel you need it. The two colors will absorb into the wood and blend into each other. As the colors are absorbed, the hard edges disappear, and you get a smooth, dark to light transition.
☐	Stain with dark walnut.
☐	Stain with colonial maple, and lightly "smear mix" with dark walnut.

Note: A very small amount of dark walnut is applied on the upper part of the lion's tongue to indicate shadow. After staining your project, make sure it has dried thoroughly before proceeding to the next step. Depending upon temperature and humidity, this can take several days.

Gluing up the project

The elevations provided are approximate and do not have to be exact. The goal is to incorporate relief in the image to provide realism. If you look at a real lion, his muzzle would be highest, because it is the part closest to you. The other segments would be glued progressively farther back and slightly elevated or recessed, to approximate a real lion's head.

The project is glued together with hot glue. Hot glue works well, because the interlocking segments provide additional structural support. Additionally, the glue can be re-melted to reposition a segment if needed. The segments are positioned together, and then a bead of hot glue is applied on the back side and along the joint. Use as much glue as you feel you need.

Step 8: Start with the lion's tongue. Hold all three segments together so that the center segment is elevated about 1/16" higher than the larger segment, and the other segment is about 1/16" higher than the center segment. While holding everything in position, turn it over and glue the pieces together.

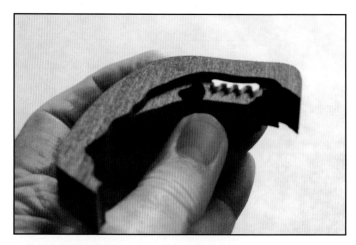

Step 9: Push the lower teeth up about 1/8" and glue them in place. While holding that assembly recessed about 1/8" below the lip segment, glue the two together.

Step 10: Position the large tooth section so it is at the same elevation as the smaller teeth, and glue it in place. Glue the two pieces of the remaining lower teeth together, then glue the section in at the same elevation as the other teeth. Fit the assembled tongue so it is recessed about ¼" below the dark lip segment, and glue it in. Glue the remaining lip segment in while it's positioned at the same elevation as the lip on the other side.

Step 11: Position and glue the small dark segment between the lip and tongue at the same elevation as the tongue. Glue the lion's upper left tooth in place at the same elevation as the other teeth. Next, glue the small segment that was stained golden oak in place on the remaining teeth. Glue the teeth to the rest of the assembly at the same elevation as the other teeth.

Step 12: Glue up the remaining sections. Use the same gluing techniques explained above. The suggested elevation for each piece is listed on the pattern, using a numbering system. Frame the completed portrait or display as is using a ring or sawtooth hanger.

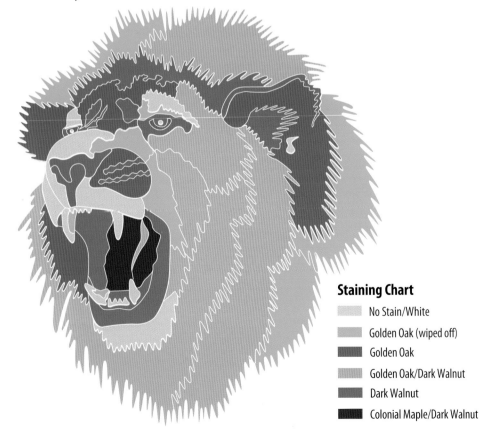

Staining Chart

	No Stain/White
	Golden Oak (wiped off)
	Golden Oak
	Golden Oak/Dark Walnut
	Dark Walnut
	Colonial Maple/Dark Walnut

Materials &Tools

Materials:
- ½" or ¾" x 12" x 14" light-colored wood of choice (I use poplar). You may need to edge glue two or more boards together to get the required dimensions.
- Two copies of the pattern (One will be used to cut the project. Save the other as a height reference when gluing.)
- Stains: golden oak, dark walnut, and colonial maple
- Two disposable aluminum baking pans (optional) and tongs for dipping segments in stain
- Selection of small artist's brushes (shading)
- Temporary-bond spray adhesive
- Waxed butcher's paper or freezer paper (to cover the work surface when staining)
- Paper towels
- Frame, ring, or sawtooth hanger

Tools:
- #3 reverse-tooth blades or blades of choice
- Drill and assorted small-diameter bits for blade-entry holes
- Hot glue gun and several sticks of hot glue
- Scissors

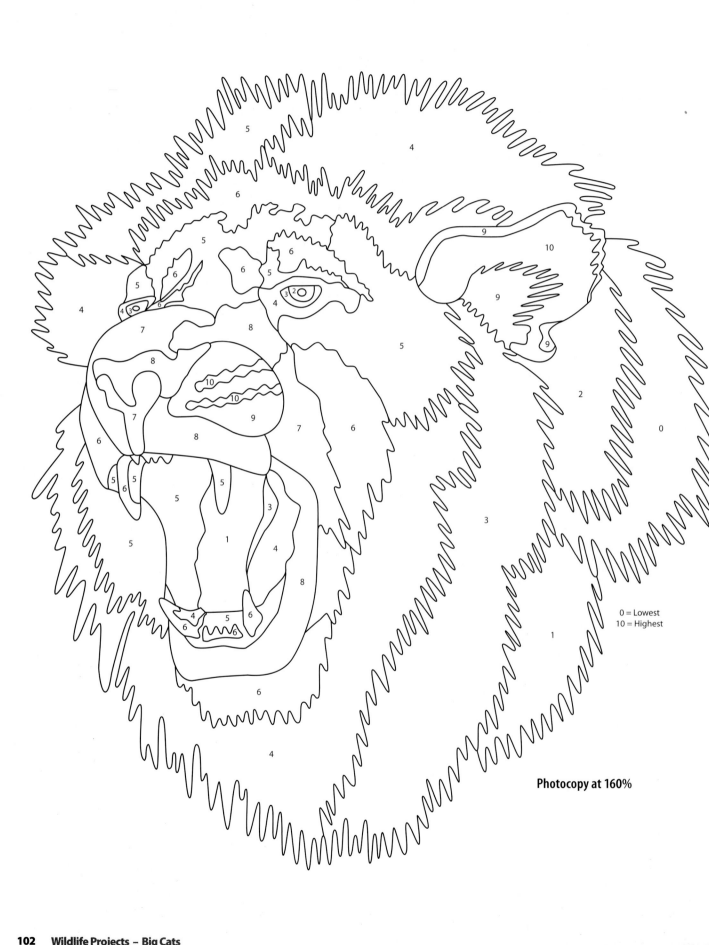

Photocopy at 160%

0 = Lowest
10 = Highest

Stalking Leopard Portrait

By Kerry Hallam

This intricate pattern is inspired by a photograph taken by Rich Adams. As soon as I saw the photo, I knew it would make a wonderful scroll saw portrait.

I immediately contacted Rich and asked permission to adapt his photo into a scroll saw pattern. Rich shared the story of the photo with me and granted me permission to use the image for a pattern. The subject, an older leopard called Big Boy, resides near the Moremi reserve in the extreme north of the Okavango Delta in Botswana. The striking image was captured as Big Boy rose from an afternoon nap to stalk closer to a few impala grazing nearby.

There are almost 1,000 frets in this pattern. You can cut the portrait from an 8" x 10" blank, but I suggest using the pattern full size and cutting the piece from an 11" x 14" blank. The larger size makes it easier to cut and gives the portrait an impressive feel worthy of this magnificent predator. I drill blade-entry holes in sets of 50 so I can move back and forth from the saw to the drill. After cutting, I use Jeff Zaffino's method to remove fuzzies from the back of the portrait: I burn them off with a small butane torch. Be careful to burn off just the fuzz and not the wood.

Materials & Tools

Materials:
- ¼" x 11" x 14" Baltic birch plywood or wood of choice
- Assorted grits of sandpaper
- Finish of choice (I use spray lacquer)

Tools:
- #2/0 spiral blades or blades of choice
- Drill with #68 drill bit (blade-entry holes)
- Butane torch (to burn off the fuzzies)

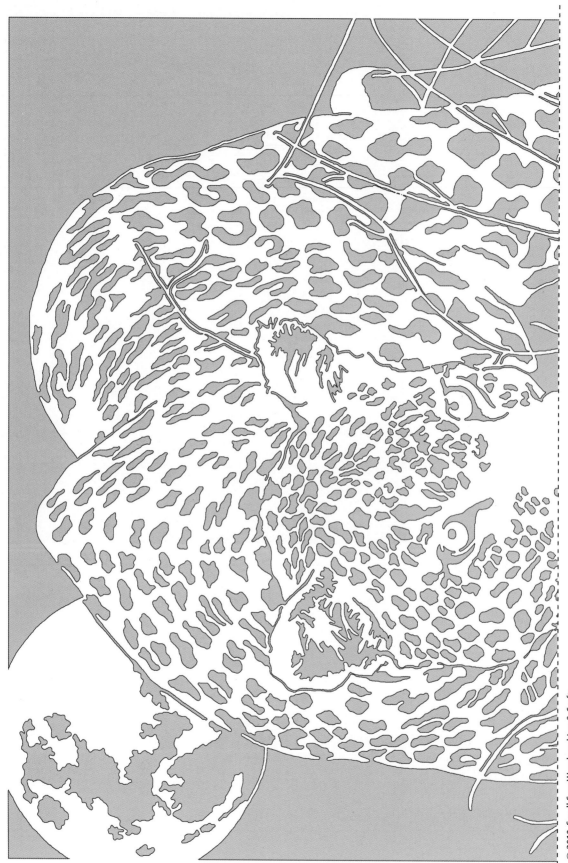

Photocopy at 125%

Photocopy at 125%

Tiger Portrait

by Charles Dearing

I specialize in designing portrait-style patterns and have found that wildlife subjects tend to be the most popular. This is a good project for scrollers just beginning to explore this style of cutting.

I cut my portraits with a spiral blade. Make your blade-entry holes with a ¹⁄₁₆"-diameter bit. Start cutting around the nose and whiskers, taping scrap pieces in place to protect fragile areas. Sand both sides of the piece carefully after cutting.

The portrait looks good with a simple clear finish, but stains and dyes can add realism to the project. Glue on your backing of choice, and frame the completed project.

Materials & Tools

Materials:
- ⅛" x 9" x 11" Baltic birch plywood or wood of choice
- ⅛" x 9" x 11" plywood painted black or backing material of choice
- Tape (to secure scrap pieces for support)
- Finish of choice
- Assorted grits of sandpaper
- Glue of choice (to attach backing)
- Frame of choice

Tools:
- #3 spiral blades or blades of choice
- Drill with ¹⁄₁₆"-diameter drill bits

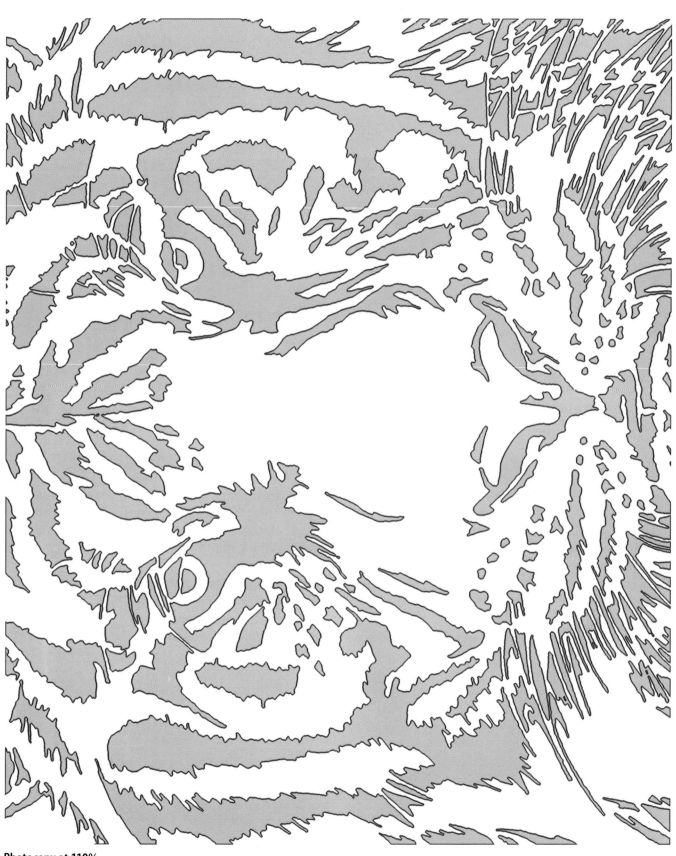

Photocopy at 110%

Hangin' Out With Mom

By Kevin Daly

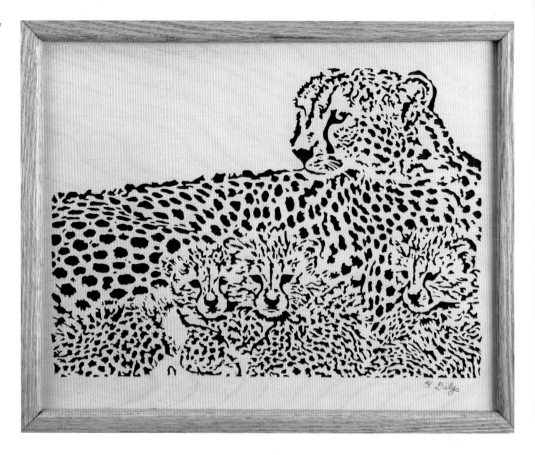

This detailed portrait is my homage to the mother cheetah protecting her cubs—I've always been a fan of big cats. This little family captured my heart—in the wild, only 1 in 10 cheetah cubs survive to adulthood.

Anyone can cut this portrait; it just takes a little patience and planning. The project, as shown, has 790 cuts. The first one I cut took me 18 hours to complete. For a less labor-intensive design, eliminate some cuts, join some holes, or just make it your own.

When using ⅛"-thick material such as this, I cut it in stacks of 4-6 pieces. This accomplishes two things: if you suffer chip-out on a piece, you still have good pieces, and it helps to reinforce the more fragile areas of the cutting.

Cover the wood and secure the stack, using blue painter's tape. Use spring clamps to secure the stack while you're taping it to make sure the stack is tight. Because the wood is covered with the tape, apply spray adhesive to the back of the pattern and the tape; this prevents the pattern from lifting off.

Drill the blade-entry holes with a #63 drill bit. I drill and cut the interior cuts in groups of 50. This allows a break from sitting at the saw, and it gives you a sense of accomplishment. Many folks prefer spiral blades for these types of patterns, but I use flat #3 reverse-tooth blades for most of my cutting. I prefer the cleaner lines and reduced finishing time from these blades. Use whichever blade you prefer.

For the backer board, I use ⅛"-thick plywood painted black. This gives the piece additional support and helps to prevent breakage. Use three coats of semi-gloss black spray paint. Once the paint is dry, rub it down with 0000 steel wool.

Lightly sand the finished portrait to remove any stray fuzzies. Use tacky glue to adhere the portrait to the backer board. Distribute weights on the top of the portrait to ensure that all of the small areas of the portrait adhere to the backer board as well. Spray the finished portrait with three coats of semi-gloss spray lacquer. Lightly hand sand the portrait with 400 to 600-grit sandpaper between coats; this gives a glass-smooth finish to the piece.

Materials & Tools

Materials:
- 2 each ⅛" x 11" x 14" Baltic birch plywood or wood of choice
- Semi-gloss black spray paint
- Semi-gloss spray lacquer or finish of choice
- Sandpaper, assorted grits
- 0000 steel wool
- Tacky glue

Tools:
- Drill with #63 drill bit
- #3 skip, reverse-tooth blades or blades of choice

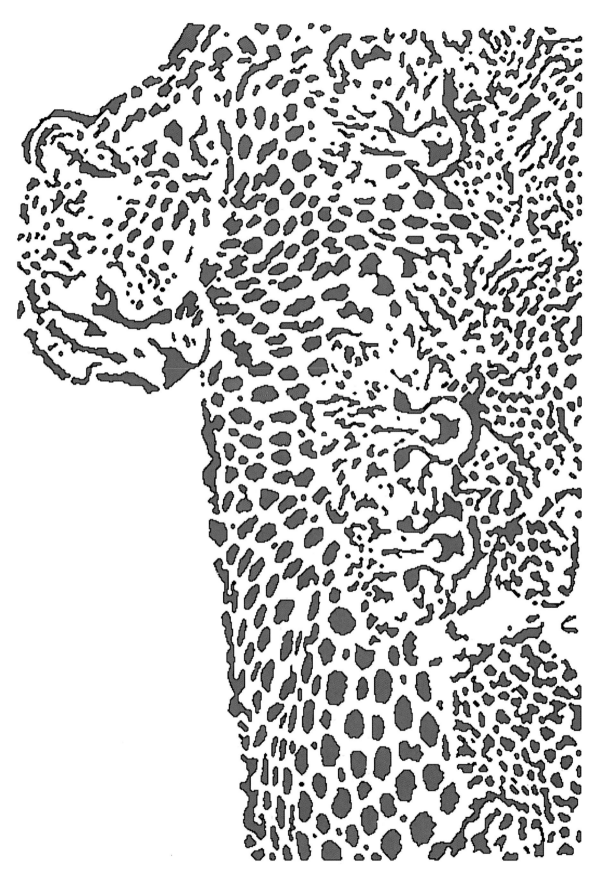

Photocopy at 150%

Jaguar Cub

By Tom Mullane

This jaguar cub is one of the more popular patterns in Tom Mullane's continuing series of wildcats. The cub's left ear and chin are slightly cut off on the edge of the pattern so the cut project can fit into a frame.

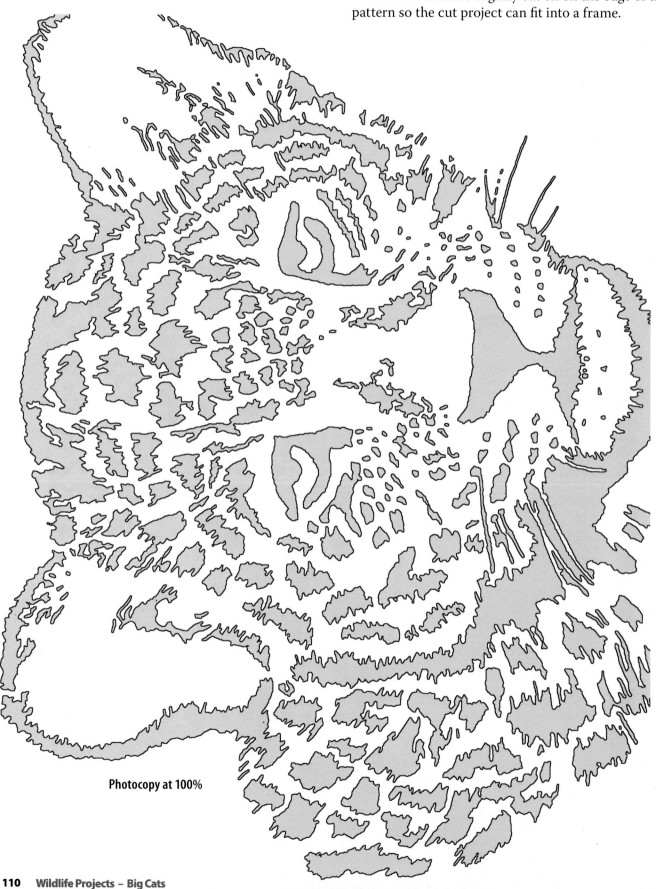

Photocopy at 100%

Contributors

Volker Arnold
Volker, of Germany, designs scroll saw patterns.
www.va-holzkunst.de

Ellen Brown
Ellen lives in Maine.

Gary Browning
Gary is known for his scrolled portraits and lives in Pennsylvania.
www.angelfire.com/md2/creativewood/browning.htm

Kevin Daly
Kevin operates K&J Woodworks in Connecticut.
www.scrollsawpatternsonline.com

Charles Dearing
Charles, of Texas, specializes in portrait-style patterns.
www.BullRunArt.com

Theresa Ekdom
Theresa lives in Michigan.
woodngoods.blogspot.com

Terry Foltz
Terry, of Washington state, specializes in wildlife, fishing, and hunting scenes.
www.scrollsaw-art.com

Kerry Hallam
Kerry, of South Carolina, retired from the Air Force and enjoys creating patterns.
kerrysbladeart.blogspot.com

Lora S. Irish
Lora, of Maryland, is a nationally-known artist and author.
www.carvingpatterns.com

Leldon Maxcy
Leldon, of Alabama, has been sawing since he was 14.
http://leldonscrollsawing.homestead.com

Neal Moore
Neal retired from the Navy in 2002. He resides in West Virginia.

Tom Mullane
Tom, of Maryland, is a scroller and designer whose work ranges from animals and cartoons to scenic pieces.
www.oldgriz.biz

John A. Nelson
John, a prolific scroller and designer, lives in New Hampshire.
www.scrollsawer.com

Deborah Nicholson
Deborah, of Hernando Beach, Fla., is a lifelong artist who has a teaching degree and often combines mediums.

Tim Rogers
Tim, of Brunswick, Ga., started designing intarsia projects in 2007.
www.intarsiabytimrogers.com

Harry Savage
Harry, of New York, enjoys scrolling portraits of people and animals.
http://harry.o.tripod.com

Tom Sevy
Tom, who lives in Utah, first encountered scroll sawing more than 50 years ago and still finds it relaxing.
www.woodyoubelieveshop.com

Janette Square
Janette, of Oregon, made her first intarsia project in 2000, and her hobby is now nearly full-time.
www.square-designs.com

Kathy Wise
Kathy is known for her intarsia work. She lives in Michigan.
www.kathywise.com

Index

Note: Page numbers in **bold** indicate projects.

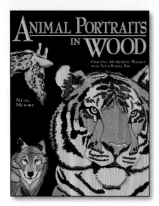
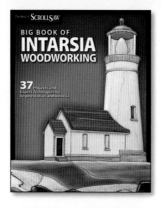
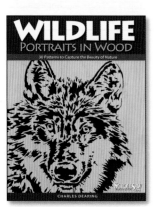
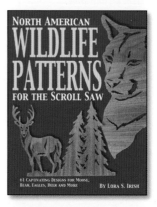
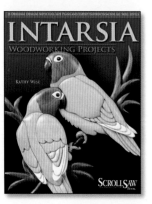
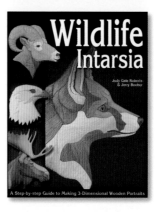